TECTONICS OF PLACE

THE ARCHITECTURE OF JOHNSON FAIN

Published in Australia in 2010 by
The Images Publishing Group Pty Ltd
ABN 89 059 734 431
6 Bastow Place, Mulgrave, Victoria 3170, Australia
Tel: +61 3 9561 5544 Fax: +61 3 9561 4860
books@imagespublishing.com
www.imagespublishing.com

National Library of Australia Cataloguing-in-Publication entry:

Author: Johnson, Scott, 1951–

Title: Tectonics of place : the architecture of Johnson Fain

ISBN: 9781864703955 (hbk)

Subjects: Johnson Fain.
           Architecture–United States–20th century.
           Architecture–United States–21st century.
           Architecture, American.

Dewey Number: 725.0973

Coordinating editor: Robyn Beaver

Designed by The Graphic Image Studio Pty Ltd, Mulgrave, Australia
www.tgis.com.au

Pre-publishing services by Mission Productions Limited, Hong Kong

Printed on 157 gsm Gold East paper by Everbest Printing Co. Ltd., in Hong Kong/China

IMAGES has included on its website a page for special notices in relation to this and our other
publications. Please visit www.imagespublishing.com.

Johnson Fain
1201 North Broadway
Los Angeles CA 90012
USA
johnsonfain.com

TECTONICS OF PLACE

THE ARCHITECTURE OF JOHNSON FAIN

images
Publishing

" Despite his claim that the selection was arbitrary, one cannot but assume he chose something just close enough to the kinds of things that were beginning to emerge as sculptural constructions, to really force the issue of what was and wasn't art, of where the realm of the aesthetic ended and where utility began."

Paul Wood, referring to Marcel Duchamp's "readymades."

Contents

Foreword

The 1970s through the 1980s was a period of civil war for architects. Post-Modernists squared off against Modernists, and then Deconstructivists against both Post-Modernists and Modernists. By the end of the decade, practicing architects, confused and exhausted by the theory wars, sought truce and a way forward.

For those unconvinced by the arguments, the default position by the early 1990s was Modernism. But practitioners keen on finding their own way hardly wanted to warm over a known quantity that was already perceived as deficient. Mies and Le Corbusier were no longer the established answers. As Scott Johnson and William Fain took over a practice established by one of Los Angeles' pre-eminent Modernists, William L. Pereira, they confronted the same questions faced by architects of their transitional generation: whither?

The wars had revealed the poverty of formalism underlying Modernism: abstraction shorn of meaning, form for form's sake, limited architecture. There was more to a building than what some Modernists called "objecthood," where the meaning of a building resided in form. Post-Modernists had criticized tabula rasa Modernism for abstracting architecture from context and history. Deconstructivists objected to Modernism's cult of objectivity, which precluded subjectivity, individuality, and the non-linear. The irrationality of Marcel Duchamp, so influential in the art world, had seeped into the awareness of architects. The way to correct form for form's sake was not to reverse the course toward informality, which was simply another form of formalism. The answer was removing form—

including structure and geometry itself—as the basic logic totalizing a building's design.

The sustained critique of Modernism provided Johnson Fain the advantage of a point of departure: the criticism was well taken and absorbed. Johnson and Fain took up their practice at a unique moment, when Modernism as a system of thought opened even as it broke. The critique cleared the way to introduce other subjects into the design process. Buildings were a vessel into which architects, as though writing a book, could pour meaning. The meaning was not the form of the vessel alone.

In architecture, the question that Scott Johnson and his colleagues at Johnson Fain faced was not so much how to reinvent Modernism, but how to devise a design process that would yield buildings that were relevant, authentic, and appropriate to the ethos of the time. The architects were not interested in espousing another "ism" and adding it to the theory wars, but instead looked to the empirical context, to the facts on the ground, to develop a basis for design. The way forward was not to follow or abandon Continental ideologies. Instead they effectively pursued the home-grown American philosophy of pragmatism, conducting research within the marketplace of commissions rather than within the more protected circumstances of academia. An empirical practice emerged. The design strategem grew by doing.

Taking advantage of a field in which ideologies were already challenged and rules broken, Johnson Fain enjoyed great operational latitude. In a remarkably prolific practice with a wide range of building types, from single-family houses to major skyscrapers, the firm has questioned assumptions on a project-by-project basis. Johnson cumulatively pyramided the results into a modus operandi that, in the practice, opened the project of Modernism from simplicity to complexity. The complexity was not merely formal. Social, urban, ecological, even anthropological issues entered the design equation.

In the extensive oeuvre, it is hard to pinpoint a single moment of epiphany that turned the firm toward a practice of widened scope. The body of commissions as a whole acted simultaneously, like a Big Bang, to provoke an enriched architecture that fulfilled Robert Venturi's promise of "complexity and contradiction" better than did the Post-Modernists. The progress was incremental but non-linear, and it mirrored ongoing questions arising in the field. Johnson Fain did not practice in isolation but treated the field as an open source of both questions and answers. The intellectual membrane between the field and the practice was porous.

The architects broke through several architectural assumptions, breaks that cleared their way for growth. Perhaps the most formidable was the notion of the whole, that ideally there should be an internally consistent logic guiding a design to a vision in which all parts agree. The tenacious idea of a whole is as old as classicism, where all parts, large to small, take their ordinated place in a hierarchy. The notion of the whole prevailed through Modernism and even Post-Modernism, but was challenged by Deconstructivists espousing a philosophy of relativism.

Johnson Fain was the beneficiary of this liberative ideology. The whole needn't be unitary. The center needn't hold. A facade could turn a corner and become something completely different just around the edge.

In downtown Dallas' Arts District, Johnson designed the high-rise residence, Museum Tower, in complex geometries that contrast with Platonic geometries of the other iconic structures in the district. The oval plan of the building intersects with the orthogonal site plan, creating an overall plan that is simultaneously linear, curvilinear, and complex. The cross section of the building is oval, necessitating an unusual application of glass as shingles, to compensate for necessary tolerances.

Towers are usually the most prescriptive building types, since the repetition of floors encourages economies that will be multiplied. As in Dallas, Johnson abandoned pure, unmutated Platonic volumes in his design of MGM Tower in Century City. In that 35-story structure, he created instead a faceted tower with several different sections top to bottom, each addressing the specifics of solar orientations, plan configurations and adjacencies. The tower was not a simple, pure shaft rising in a single thrust, but a composite of different floor plates, programs, and facades differentiated by respective patterns of glass and granite. Form ceded to surface as varying patterns responded to circumstance. The universal gave way to the local.

Modernism was greatly influenced by the logic of industrialization, which assumed assembly-line production for a mass market of averaged conditions and a normative population. In architecture, architects generalized a single solution into a typical solution, universally applicable: design a better window, produce it industrially, and everyone benefits collectively from a cumulatively improved environment. What resulted from this basically industrial logic was standardization, and the loss of individuality in both the building and the concept of the user.

Universality and standardization reinforced the concepts of purity and the whole, but as Johnson focuses increasingly on the particulars of a commission, the specificities gradually gather momentum as a generative idea eroding the monolithic unity that has typified many Modernist buildings.

Sometimes the application of specificity is simple and at a small scale. In a townhouse in Los Angeles, where abstract white living spaces flow into one another, Johnson planted exceptional architectural events, such as abstractly sculpted fireplaces and bookcases, which mark moments in an otherwise homogeneous interior. At the larger scale of MetLofts in Downtown Los Angeles, the architects accepted the mixed-use program and designed a building that expresses rather than suppresses its heterogeneity. With townhouses, lofts, retail and public space, the courtyard building takes on a fine-grain texture as a result of the straightforward, unvarnished expression of its constituent parts. In this case the patterns are more than expressions of surface: they are rooted in program. The facade also responds to its context, an intensely urban section of downtown to which the densely differentiated facade contributes

its own dose of urban energy. The architects are responding to program, place and circumstance. The building is not an absolute object but a resultant of interior and exterior forces.

Even though MetLofts is a protected community with a concierge at a desk, the architects do not treat the building as a self-contained object but open it to the city to invite the city and its energies into the project. A wide passage from the street leads into a courtyard lined with apartments and social spaces. A large and inviting glass-fronted lobby also brings the streetscape into the building, and vice versa: passersby glimpse the life inside. Johnson is applying California, and Modernist, concepts of domestic indoor/outdoor flow to the city in a way that urbanizes the building. The building reciprocates, architecturalizing the streetscape, maximizing retail and live/work townhouses along the street. The building program is deployed to energize the project and animate the street. The physical object melts into the energies of the city to which it contributes its share.

Social engineering, then, has entered Johnson Fain's repertoire of design considerations. As in MetLofts, the architects have programmed the courtyard of a Los Angeles high school to cultivate edges of activity that humanize the school. They place the programs that can be open to the outside, such as the cafeteria and workshops, so that the inside edge of the courtyard school, populated and active, socializes the environment and animates public space. A building typology that in Los Angeles has classically been suburbanized with lawns and landscaping is now urbanized. Parts within a building matrix that have usually been standardized are now differentiated. Johnson Fain cultivates difference and variety rather than homogeneity and uniformity.

If the architects invite the city into their urban buildings, they invite the landscape into their suburban and rural structures as well. Architectural space as conceived at Johnson Fain is not contained and isolated. The architects design their buildings to participate in their surroundings, hybridizing the building and landscape. They have designed a number of technology campuses, and even when the programs require encapsulated space, they contextualize the buildings in landscapes whose character inflects the projects. Inside the suburbanized blocks, they urbanize the public spaces by programming corridors and courtyards with activities that socialize the environments. The environments are hybrids of urban and suburban, public and private space.

Johnson has made a specialty of designing wineries, and as in the urban buildings that melt into the city, these structures melt into the landscape. They do not dominate. He opens forms so that they merge into topography, the object taking on the subjectivity of a landscape that has been valorized since the pastoral poets of antiquity. Vineyards occupy a special place in the Western cultural psyche, and Johnson parses his buildings into the vineyards. The building is not an object on the landscape, but a subject within it.

Nowhere is a building more fused with the land than in the firm's design for the American Indian Cultural Center and Museum in Oklahoma City, where the building grows into and out of the site in a sweeping spiral berm. Here Johnson Fain's design taps into the mythic power of the landscape. The firm's architects and planners conducted a sustained study of the culture of local Indians, and the museum that houses their culture acknowledges the Indian affinity to the four basic elements, especially the earth. The building is not a neutral vessel, but one impregnated with the meaning of the culture of its subjects. The architects did not design a symbol of Indian culture, but embodied its belief system in their design.

Additively, project by project, the architects have addressed issues and absorbed lessons that have broadened the range of subjects, from the obvious to the arcane: from urbanism and the landscape to poetry and myth. The result is not just formal complexity, or complexity as style, but complexity as a way of elasticizing a more narrow interpretation of the profession into an embracing cultural practice.

For Johnson Fain notions of formal modernist purity and regularity have ceded to plays between structure and what Johnson calls "improvisation." The Johnson Fain practice oscillates in a fluctuating and indeterminate zone between the linear and nonlinear, objective and subjective, universal and local, standard and exceptional, homogenous and heterogeneous. For all its social aspirations, Modernism was confined by its pledges of regularity, purity and structure. It therefore tended to closure as a system of thinking. Through a capacious and generous process of intellectual synthesis, Johnson Fain expands architecture beyond building into an open practice of thought.

—*Joseph Giovannini*

Introduction

Johnson Fain was formed at the end of the 1980s and evolved out of the William L. Pereira office, a Los Angeles-based architecture and planning firm practicing worldwide. Well-known and large in its prime, the Pereira practice addressed itself to growing post-World War II industries that included aerospace, television and motion pictures, educational buildings and university campuses, new town development, and resorts and recreational facilities. After some years of study and practice on the East Coast, my partner, Bill Fain, a Southern California native, and I, a Northern Californian, each returned to Los Angeles and, following Bill Pereira's death, we jointly assumed control of the office. I continued in the role of leading the design of architecture and interiors as I had done since relocating from New York, while Bill came to oversee the urban design and planning efforts as well as most of the management within our new firm.

Whereas the work of the Pereira practice was central to the suburban expansion of its time, we, at Johnson Fain, emerged during a period of revived interest in the city. We had moved back to California from major Atlantic cities and were a part of the next generation drawn to dense urban development, mixed-use design, verticality, infill building, public transportation and its impacts, open space, the idea of urban ecologies, and the shifting and tenuous relationships between public and private power within the city. The Pereira work was often noted for a kind of idealism, an expressive optimism in the future, and a premise that buildings and master plans of scale implied a broad consensus. Johnson Fain work appeared in the region later, finding urban communities more diverse and factional where physical outcomes were complex and frequently negotiated among multiple parties. In this context, our design work has often reflected that exchange: open grids that are tied to a specific place but allow flexibility and expansion over time, buildings that display fluid and sometimes ambiguous relations with a redefined ground plane and sense of territory. While the Pereira firm, in its architecture, often worked to achieve drama by way of a geometric and monumental iconography, we at Johnson Fain pursue an iconic architecture by way of movement, attention to surfaces, hybrid unions, and a sense of the provisional. These, we have felt, are the physical realities of our own time.

Over the approximately two decades of our design work, we have been fortunate to work on design projects that range from furnishings to large-scale master plans. The focus of this book is the making of architecture at Johnson Fain and its relationship to the creation of place. Thus the title, Tectonics of Place. Within that focus, it must be said that we view architecture as a unified design process that joins the crafts of creating architecture and interior space. All physical design requires artful attention to place, circumstance, time, and the particular needs of a sponsor. We believe it is from this that unique architecture grows.

TALL BUILDINGS + URBAN HABITATS

The first architectural commission for what soon became Johnson Fain was the 34-story headquarters tower for the 20th Century Fox Film Corporation. Commissioned in late 1983 and completed in 1987, the building is sited in Century City, California at the topographic high point

1   2   3   4   5   6

of the Fox studio lot on a narrow slice of land on axis with Olympic Boulevard to the west. While the general neighborhood included other tall buildings, the mix of land uses, from low-rise residential buildings to mid-rise hotels to single-family dwellings and retail, left us with very little sense of uniform context. Located at the intersection of Century City's two predominant streets, our commission held the promise of refocusing the area with the addition of a new tall building. Fox Plaza became an iconic and self-referential tower visible from all directions. We employed oblique glass planes to reflect light in ways that articulate the building's sculptural shapes. Beginning with a square plan, we rotated an equivalent square forty-five degrees off the first, creating a highly faceted shaft that was clad in complex patterns of glass and granite varying over the height of the building. This interest in surface and patterning was the beginning of an ongoing idea that provided us a bridge from a kind of Postmodern decorative strategy to more refined and modern surfaces in later buildings.

Additional commissions for tall buildings followed after the opening of Fox Plaza, among them, 1999 Avenue of the Stars, later to be renamed SunAmerica Center; Rincon Center, a mixed-use twin tower project in San Francisco; the Nestlé USA headquarters in Glendale; and Los Angeles Center, a master plan and twin tower design on the former Union Oil of California (UNOCAL) property in downtown Los Angeles. The Trump Organization called from New York and engaged us to study the former and historic Ambassador Hotel site as a mixed-use urban village with super-tall towers in the heart of the Wilshire Boulevard corridor.

Much of the large-scale work that included tall buildings slowed throughout the 1990s. Although the market for urban space eventually returned, many years passed before large vacancies in existing buildings were absorbed. In the meantime, we began to expand our work overseas and opportunities presented themselves for us to do significant planning work in China, which created the occasional opportunity to propose tall buildings and highly dense developments there. Locally, we were frequently commissioned to redesign or provide substantial upgrades to existing tall buildings, among them, 10880 Wilshire Boulevard, Union Bank Plaza, Pacific Corporate Towers, the Pacific Mutual Building, 600, 626, 707, and 1100 Wilshire Boulevard in downtown Los Angeles, as well as 5900 Wilshire Boulevard opposite the Los Angeles County Museum of Art.

During this time of weak demand for new tall buildings in America, JMB Realty Corp., our former client for SunAmerica Center and the owner of vacant lands in Century City, commissioned us to design yet another high-rise office tower, which became the headquarters for Metro-Goldwyn-Mayer. The building contains a broad, low bustle that includes the floors of the low-rise elevator bank. MGM required large floorplates and wished to control elevator access to all of its floors. Above, the building narrows and climbs as a vertical extrusion to the top floor. The tower is broadly curved on two opposing ends, softening the shape and creating radiating views from within. We worked on the window-wall to create a highly reticulated surface of diagonally organized panels of glass chevrons and recessed frames. Columns on the ground floor are wrapped in

7

8

9

10   11   12

fractal stone covers and the glass wall of the lobby is hung from above, which allowed us to maintain an all-glass storefront looking into the garden outside.

The first decade of the new millennium brought to us a wide range of tall urban building commissions, some built and others stalled in the financial contractions that began in 2008. Metropolitan Lofts is a highly dense concrete building of only eight stories that completed construction in 2006 in downtown Los Angeles. For a third time, JMB Realty Corp. commissioned us to design tall buildings, this time two 47-story residential towers in Century City, while other commissions included tall buildings in San Diego, Glendale, Anaheim, Hollywood, downtown Los Angeles, Osaka, Japan, and Dallas, Texas.

Museum Tower is planned for a site on Flora Street at the center of Dallas' Arts District. It is designed to be the only vertical building in a neighborhood that includes the Dallas Museum of Art, the Nasher Sculpture Gallery, the Morton H. Meyerson Symphony Hall, the Wyly Theater, the Winspear Opera Hall, and the Booker T. Washington High School for the Performing and Visual Arts. It appeared to us that the many distinguished architects of the neighborhood had designed their buildings from a set of late-modern sculptural forms; all are variations on Platonic solids. There are no mutated forms or hyperbolic surfaces. Even the latest among them, the opera hall and theater, are simple forms. Taking this up as the general unifier of the place, we designed a 42-story glass tower that becomes an oval in plan and a very subtle oval in cross-section. We designed the window panels to be glass shingles, which allow us

to approximate the oval curves with facets. The long ends of the tower are left open and designed as deep shaded terraces. A range of glass coatings coded to the activities within the residences are used to animate the surface of the tower and create a seemingly random pattern of varying transparencies and opacity.

During this period of high activity, we purchased a building in downtown Los Angeles' Chinatown, substantially remodeled it and moved into it as our own interdisciplinary design studio. The long, low building, formerly one of LA's earliest automobile showrooms, was reclad and redesigned to open up the sky-lit volumes of this bow-truss building. Located on a bend in the Los Angeles River at the foot of Elysian Park, our site is at the northern edge of downtown and a few steps from the original eighteenth-century encampment of Gaspar de Portolá, one of California's first European explorers.

PASTORAL LANDSCAPES

Opus One was, for us, a unique and early opportunity to explore the relative borders of building and landscape. Also, issues of culture in the form of architectural semantics quickly became part of our design brief. While Baron Philippe de Rothschild and his daughter, the Baroness Philippine, were refreshingly modern, and Robert Mondavi was a Californian rooted in his own time and place, architectural forms became signifiers of different things to different members of the client team. European quality to some, a Romantic Classical tradition best known in France to others. A modern sculpture in stone, timber, and bronze for some, a futuristic intervention by others. While the plan and section of the

13

14

15

16

17

18

building are highly functional and modern, the choice of finish materials and architectural style became a fusion of the goals of the two families: a signifier for one and an aspirational symbol for the other.

The winery is set deep into the Napa Valley floor with a broad berm covering and insulating the crescent-shaped first-year barrel cellar. Social and activity spaces overhead surround the semi-enclosed garden and quiet forecourt as a part of the arrival sequence. The valley floor runs up and over the berm, capped by a simple cornice, establishing the roof-level belvedere as the top of a mound that encases the building. Native oak and redwood, domestic limestone and local concrete aggregates were employed to ground the winery in a familiar rendition of nature.

Soon thereafter, we were invited to work with Ernest Gallo and his family on a series of proposals for a winery and visitors center in the foothills of Sonoma's 7,000-acre Frei Ranch. Here, we experimented with the abstraction of topography by recreating the elevational lines of the hillside site, much as one would read a topographic map. These lines became curvilinear stone walls embedded in the hill, their capstones striking simple horizontal lines against the verticality of tree trunks that would surround and occasionally penetrate the glassy structure.

Other winery proposals include many studies for both a large Central California winery for the Robert Mondavi Coastal brand in the Salinas Valley, and the Donum Estate winery in Carneros for the German vintner Marcus Moller-Racke. One study explores pure linear abstraction as a representation of the linear process of winemaking

(receiving, stemming/crushing, fermentation, barreling, bottling, and shipping), while the other addresses "gravity flow" in small tank lots for custom pinot noir blending. At Donum, operations and guest services are fused into a linear building embedded into a hill.

The Byron Winery commissioned us to create a new building in 1993 after Robert Mondavi Winery purchased the venture and 640 acres located at the northern edge of Santa Barbara County. The site lies within one of the many central coastal valleys of California open to the Pacific Ocean and is bordered by spare, rolling hills. The winery, oriented north/south, is set into the ground on a mild slope, which allows fruit delivery to be loaded with the aid of gravity into the fermentation cellar from the easterly uphill grade. Conversely, the westerly downhill side opens up the activity spaces to the ground plane, views of the vineyards, and the cooling wind and western sunsets. The building's roofline and volume take the shape of a horizontal extrusion and have been planned for future expansion. The major building materials are wide cedar planks and battens, integrally colored hand plaster, and rolled zinc sheet stock. The building's form is meant to recall the rolling forms of the hills that provide nature's backdrop.

Much of the early 1990s was spent in the master planning and design of the LeoPalace Resort in Manenggon Hills, Guam. We established a local office there in order to oversee the detailed coordination and construction of what was to become a two-square-mile recreational resort for a well-known Japanese homebuilder. Housing of various types, recreational clubs, amenities, and

a hotel and village were designed and constructed around a lake and 45 holes of golf. Located in the Mariana Islands, the project is set in a challenging tropical climate with a 400-year heritage of Spanish history. Solid concrete construction and tile roofs are employed for stability and typhoon resistance while balconies and deep eaves provide shade and capture winds off the Philippine Sea and Pacific Ocean. This work ultimately led to detailed proposals for resorts in Saipan, Australia, and China, as well as completed golf clubs in Los Angeles, Barbados, and Napa.

A unique and long-term project, which came to us in 1996 and is still in construction, is the American Indian Cultural Center and Museum (AICCM). The commission began as a site selection process for a Native American cultural center that acknowledges Oklahoma's diverse American Indian population. An intense master planning and programming effort followed, which involved workshops with representatives of the many tribes and concept design for multiple parts of the plan. Recreational fields, pow-wow grounds, wetland discovery areas, hospitality zones, artists' village, and the centrally located AICCM building were all sited and designed. Highly collaborative between Oklahomans, Native Americans, architects, landscape architects, planners and programmers, building engineers, and exhibition designers, the architecture of the cultural center took on unpredictable yet iconic formal language that merges landscape and building in the extreme. Native American elements of nature (water, wind, earth, and fire) are threaded through the arrival sequence of the design from the entry gate to the interior of the

great circular promontory. Native American habitats of forest, plain, and river are generative themes of the master plan landscape. The location of building elements within the circular berm recreates a sundial, marking the seasonal variations in sunrise and sunset.

Once known as Oklahoma's first oil drilling site, the property was given to the Native American Cultural and Educational Authority requiring toxic remediation and taking on the familiar Native American theme of "healing the earth." Major building elements of the project are the Great Promontory, Court of Nations, Court of the Wind, and Hall of the People. The primary mission of the project and its exhibition contents is to give a full accounting of Native American history. Needless to say, this is a commission that has required a considerable learning curve and has been exploratory and collaborative among all parties.

TECHNOLOGY, EDUCATION + RESEARCH

For nearly a decade and a half, we have had the good fortune to work with Amgen, the Thousand Oaks, California-based biotechnology giant, in designing and developing much of its 120-acre campus. We have designed multiple buildings, a wide variety of interior environments, site amenities, parking, a system of outdoor public spaces, and landscape. Most of this work has been done with the encouragement and under the watchful eye of Kevin Sharer, Amgen's energetic CEO. From the beginning, our design efforts have been focused on the integration of indoor and outdoor space and the quality of the working environment overall as well as the design excellence of individual buildings.

22   23   24   25

Our design efforts began with the first office building in the administrative headquarters of the campus on an elevated site that eventually became a highly programmed garden surrounded by Amgen's three principal buildings. Outdoor circulation grids trace their way through lobbies and between buildings, encouraging cross-campus pedestrian movement and connecting a wide range of open spaces and campus amenities. Established garden and plan typologies create consistency and bone structure through the growing campus, while unique buildings, gardens, and recreational centers provide variety. Working on a large site for a decade and a half has proven to be a spectacular opportunity both to extend the values of a community in physical form over time and to learn from each effort and evolve.

Various projects for Genentech, Northern California's biotechnology leader, followed. At Genentech, we have been involved in performing a wide range of site studies, and, like Amgen, determining ways to design strategic infill in a manner that adds capacity to the existing building stock while improving common areas and amenities. Indoor and outdoor spaces are fused together while buildings are carefully sited with respect to views of the San Francisco Bay, natural light, and the wind patterns of the peninsula. Genentech has just merged with Roche, the major European pharmaceutical company and will now, no doubt, undergo further transformation.

Several other large campuses suited to modern technology companies came our way, starting with the headquarters for Experian in Costa Mesa and The Horizon for Lincoln Property Company in Playa Vista.

In the case of Experian, a worldwide credit data and marketing company, security is paramount and yet the flat site and local weather called for openness, long view corridors, comfortable circulation patterns, and generous landscape. A secure outside perimeter is established with four finger buildings radiating from a large central garden. Amenities such as cafeteria and employee services hug the central garden, as do all the elevator lobbies, which provide views into the garden. The Horizon was an exercise in designing within a highly defined urban framework that had been established both by the precedent of nearby historic buildings and by a set of design guidelines for the new community of Playa Vista. Five low-rise buildings with enormous floorplates wrap around courtyards and are clad in a complex range of exterior skins. One is a straightforward expression of the concrete column and beam structure that provides support. The other is a highly layered rainscreen of variously coated and perforated sheet metals, sunshades, and translucent window transoms designed to respond to different solar orientations. Expressing the innate abilities of a building to provide energy management at its exterior skin became the core of the design concept. The large checkerboard pattern celebrated, for us, the importance of the building's envelope.

The worlds of private-sector science and the university have grown closer over the past two decades. Historically, a bright line was drawn between the purely academic science of the university environment and the commercially driven world of science startups. But Silicon Valley changed that forever. The intersection of formerly separate natural and applied sciences (physics, biology,

26

27

28

29

chemistry, engineering, computer science), as well as the cooperation of leaders in both the private sector and university-based research, portends the future.

Recently, multiple campuses within the University of California system were given substantial grants from the State to construct interdisciplinary centers for scientific research and collaboration. These new programs are referred to as the Centers for Information Technology Research in the Interest of Society (CITRIS) and have become the basis for a series of new campus buildings. At the University of California at Irvine, Johnson Fain was commissioned to design the California Institute of Telecommunications and Information Technology, or Cal(IT)[2]. Intended to provide flex research, clean room, and office space for graduate students, faculty, fellows, invited private sector scientists, and engineers, the building also provides casual and formal meeting spaces, lecture halls and an amphitheatre. A significant portion of the building program is dedicated to the intersection of applied science and the arts and social sciences. A media laboratory is located at the center of the project to document and relay progress on a wide range of experimental research efforts.

We then were commissioned to design a second CITRIS facility, this time an expansion to Davis Hall at the University of California at Berkeley. Renamed Sutardja Dai Hall, this new building hugs the existing Davis Hall South and accommodates interdisciplinary research and production in the field of nanotechnology. Again, flex research, clean rooms, and office space are included with elaborate support services for program participants.

The Marvell Nanofabrication Laboratory was designed to include the world's most advanced semiconductor fabrication equipment. Electronic microchips will be produced in the laboratory at resolutions 100,000 times smaller than the diameter of a human hair. In addition to providing space whose use may evolve over time, the building is also a dense infill project in an increasingly dense neighborhood within the campus. Building edges are glazed and accessible adjacent to courtyard, gardens, and arcades, and the project has become as much a definer of exterior open space and functionality as a container of highly specialized programs within.

While we were busy designing for these two institutions of higher learning, we were also producing a substantial redesign for the Student Services Center at Pasadena's Fuller Theological Seminary, a sciences and performing arts addition to the Marlborough School in central Los Angeles, and the Playa Vista Community Library. All projects emphasize accessibility, sustainability, natural light, and connectivity to important pre-existing conditions.

In 1997, voters in Los Angeles County passed Bond Proposition BB to upgrade existing public schools and construct new neighborhood schools. The Los Angeles Unified School District (LAUSD) was the recipient of substantial funding and began an ambitious plan to locate sites for new schools throughout the region. Johnson Fain was commissioned to design both the 19-acre downtown high school known today as the Miguel Contreras Learning Complex and North Hollywood's 7-acre Roy Romer Middle School, named for the former Governor of Colorado and subsequently, the

30

31

32

33

Superintendent of the LAUSD who oversaw the vast building program. Both projects are sited in highly urban environments, bordered by busy arterial streets and mixed-use communities. Miguel Contreras is among the largest schools in the District with accommodations for 1,900 students, an auditorium seating 800, one gymnasium each for young men and women, basketball courts, track and field facilities, a baseball diamond, and an Olympic-size swimming pool. The site is bisected by a major automobile thoroughfare, which required the design of a pedestrian bridge, and serves to segregate the program into two blocks: one city block for the academic, auditorium, media center and food service, and the majority of the other block for all athletic programs. Security and visibility are important in this urban school, and public elements of the program are located near the entry gate surrounding a large courtyard to encourage community interaction. All circulation space is covered but open-air and naturally ventilated, while gardens were designed to encourage outdoor teaching and studies.

The Roy Romer Middle School is a slightly smaller school wherein public elements of the program are similarly located near the entrance, wrapping a generous plaza for community activities. An academic bar building runs along the major boulevard with athletic buildings located to the rear, adjacent to playing fields. Again, circulation spines are covered and naturally ventilated with views out to a range of courtyards, plazas, and lawn pads. Like the high school, building materials are familiar and highly durable. A preponderance of concrete block, corrugated and perforated steel panels, exposed structural steel stairs and framing elements, rolling glass garage doors, and brightly painted plaster make up the majority of building elements.

HOUSES

Over the past 15 years, we have, from time to time, taken on the design of private residences. Generally, we have declined the commissions for houses for a variety of reasons. It has been my experience that, on the whole, there is a small percentage of houses being commissioned that align with our objectives for the work. In the US, for example, there are a great many individuals with the means to build their own homes. Quite naturally, they bring with that prospect an accumulated sense of expectation. Questions of sentiment, tradition, opulence, style, and courage hover over these commissions. In California, it may be a fondness for all things Mediterranean, a romanticized Mission history, or, as I have long wondered, a local culture of cinematic storytelling that results in few commissions promising something modern and authentic. Secondly, of course, is the nature of the challenge that faces our clients. Those of us who have been through the process of designing and constructing a single-family residence know the complexity of the process, the need to attend to minute detail, and the importance of patience and rationality in a process that can be taxing. Spiking commodity prices, design review committees, non-performing subcontractors, and the necessary personal introspection that attend the design of a good house can all have a grinding effect on our homeowner. An architect can reasonably look at the prospective client at the outset and ask whether the person, the couple, or the family has ever been through a similar process. Will they have the patience and stamina to survive it?

Challenges noted, we began our residential work with a significant remodel in Cheviot Hills, California for a prominent attorney and his wife in the early 1990s. Our client's law practice had expanded and he moved it into our SunAmerica Center in nearby Century City when he asked us to redesign his home to accommodate the couple whose grown children would visit but not live in the home. By the time our contractor had opened up the house to expand rooms, add amenities and rework the gardens, the existing building had been taken down to the subfloor, footings, and chimney. Everything was rebuilt from there. A series of interlocking grids brought the rooms back together into a semblance of the existing house with all spaces, save the bedrooms and bathrooms, open to the interior. A big radial stairway anchors the house vertically and is lined in stair-stepped panels of stained cherry.

At a similar time and following a number of years working on the Opus One Winery in the Napa Valley, my wife and I purchased 60 acres above the town of St. Helena. This precipitous site was located high in the Mayacamas Mountains at the end of a dead-end road above White Sulphur Springs, one of the valley's four historic thermal hot springs. Set upon a mildly sloping spit of land surrounded on three sides by ravines, the house was designed as a series of cedar boxes running along the center of the site, and pulled apart at strategic moments to admit sunlight and particular views. The 200-foot length of the house slowly descends the topography for about seven feet from the entrance to the living room. Broad flagstone landings and small clusters of steps create functional zones within the house and terminate at the living room, which is anchored by two fireplaces and three walls of glass. Beyond, the site progresses from porch to descending lawn to pool, vineyard, and oak forest.

Not long after the house was finished, I was introduced to another prominent attorney, this time from San Francisco. He had built several modern homes and had been an investor in various winery ventures in the Napa Valley. He visited our St. Helena home and asked us to design one for him on a 42-acre site across the valley in Rutherford and set into the hillside above the inn, L'Auberge du Soleil. The site is gently sloped with a flat portion at the top, removed from the resort below, and scattered with limestone boulders. Scrub oaks blanket the site and drift downhill, giving the house an attractive seclusion.

As a home for an adult couple, we were asked to design a focused and private house with a very open plan. Because of the surrounding oak forest and the falling grade, large portions of the house could be opened up with wide expanses of glass without sacrificing privacy. In the end, the house became two solid containers at opposite ends of a wide glass bridge. The solids are, on one end, a study and exercise room, and on the other end, a kitchen, a large master bedroom suite, and a home office, while the glass bridge is a transparent rectangle that includes the living and dining rooms. A long concrete plank defines the entry to the house as it dodges boulders and native grasses, leading the eye through the glass bridge to the linear pool, scrub oak, and valley view beyond.

39   40   41   42   43

Sometime thereafter, I received a call from another couple requesting a conversation concerning their family's home in Malibu, California. At the time, they were leasing a large, glassy home in the Malibu hills overlooking the Pacific Ocean not far from the site where they had been burned out of their original home in a recent coastal fire. Nearby was a large sloping site from which, on a clear day, one could see Point Dume to the west and the Santa Monica Pier to the east. A long driveway led to a small stout building that enclosed a four-car garage with a generous living unit above. The family soon moved onto the property and asked us to design a house that would be built while they lived on site.

Entry to the house is at the top of the hill and requires one to arrive at a higher level, stepping down one floor to the living and family spaces, which open out to the deck, pool, gardens, and ocean views. The bedrooms are located on the upper floor, which the entry vestibule bisects: master bedroom suite on the right and the bedrooms for their boys on the left. Bedroom views are elevated with a precise placement of windows while the lower floor is fully glazed and accessible to the outside. The entry sequence, which includes a grand stair and living room, is shaped as a tall glass drum, providing a hinge around which the wings of the house wander against the bend of the hill behind.

In 1998, a different kind of challenge presented itself. A young Silicon Valley executive and his wife approached us to visit a 12-acre hilltop site they had just acquired in Los Altos Hills in Northern California. At the end of a long and winding driveway stood a derelict steel house, windows broken, building frame charred, and gardens gone to seed. We came to understand that the couple had purchased the house with the ambition to restore and expand the building to suit the needs of their young and growing family. Noting that an all-steel home in the San Francisco Bay Area was exceptional, a little research revealed that the original house was designed in 1958 by John Funk, an accomplished regional modernist who practiced during the same period as John Entenza's Case Study program in Southern California. Clearly, Funk had been influenced by this movement and laid out a beautiful and practical plan landscaped by Robert Royston, our landscape architect for Opus One, and published in Sally Woodbridge's seminal 1988 book *Bay Area Houses*.

We expanded the house in the direction of its length, adding capacity to both the garage and the grandparents' living quarters. Much of the original core of the house was preserved in plan, although the family room and kitchen were expanded with the addition of broad outdoor terraces and a fireplace set against the garden. The original modest bedroom was expanded into a master bedroom suite with a nearby children's suite of bedrooms cloistered around a playroom. The gardens, including a vegetable garden for the children, were designed by Nancy Power to be highly usable.

The house uses little manufactured energy for climate control as we installed large operable hoppers in many of the windows, which are shaded by deep overhangs in the flat roof. Long skylights, aimed to the north and lined in sycamore, bounce light into the rooms below. Forced-air systems were banished as the house relies on a radiant

concrete floor system throughout for both hot and cold ambient temperatures. Air movement is managed through the operable sashes, which are generously distributed around the perimeter of the house.

After some years of living in an existing house in central Los Angeles and finding my young teenage children approaching the age of mobility and a certain independent attitude, my wife and I determined to design and build a more urban home in a mixed-use community where we would be within walking distance to major goods and services. While this is old news in many older American communities, Los Angeles has clung strangely and persistently to a suburban model of the single-family house, made only marginally habitable by complete reliance on the automobile. We located and purchased a commercial site on Larchmont Boulevard, the town center of Hancock Park in central Los Angeles, and proceeded to design our next residence. Zoning administrators were perplexed, having apparently forgotten that it was legal to down-zone a site from commercial to residential property "as-of-right." Even as the issue of legality was cleared up, they remained perplexed, failing to understand why one would choose to build a custom home on a compact commercial site. Fortunately, now with the revival of much of downtown Los Angeles' historic core and the more urban development activities of cities such as Hollywood, Santa Monica, and Culver City, attitudes have evolved quickly in the past decade. Still, an array of codes and zoning protocols lag behind.

Once underway, we subtracted all property setbacks and designed a three-story box building that slips snugly into the urban site. The simple volume was cut-out, curved, and glazed both to address varying conditions of privacy and views and to control the admission of natural light and heat during various times of the day. Vertically, the house is zoned to provide service and support at the ground level: laundry, housekeeping, garage, wine cellar, media room, potting shed, and three gardens. The front garden is a fully paved outdoor room with a large steel table set among canopy trees and wrapped by a six-foot hedge. To the rear is the flower garden that includes water, a pergola, and sitting areas. Along the 80 feet of the sunny south side yard is the winter garden where my wife plants winter vegetables and squashes, giving way to herbs, beans, artichokes, tomatoes, eggplants, and grapes in the summer. At the second level of the house are located living, dining, and kitchen to the front, master bedroom to the rear. Tall windows with shades facing south and west can be adjusted to admit or exclude sunlight and heat. On the third, and top, floor is the children's bedrooms and baths, a study room, library, and rooftop terraces. We clung to the theory that if my wife and I lived here alone one day, most everything would be at hand to us on the second level. The house would accommodate change.

CIVIC SPACE

What constitutes civic space is a concern for all designers of the public realm. The question is a particularly complex one in a world where public/private partnerships are common tools to achieve public policy goals with the significant participation of private entities. In the marketing of large private sector projects, quasi-public commercial space is frequently created to lure the public

46   47   48

into the kinds of spaces that the public sector fails to offer. To the degree that public space is designed to serve an increasingly diverse population, the design of a kind of civility that encourages pride, accommodates plurality, and supports interaction is vital. Within our design studio, we say that, "every project of scale is, to some degree, a public project." In the best of the large private projects, this attitude allows new buildings to be seamless with the public realm and to connect to the larger structure of the city.

Rincon Center is an example of a private project that required public access and identity in order for it to succeed as an urban space. A large mixed-use project, Rincon Center includes the adaptive re-use of the historic Rincon Postal Annex, an addition of two floors of office, exterior gardens and plazas, and new office and residential towers. The ground plane is completely accessible to the public and infused with retail and restaurant tenants. We designed a central gallery through the original building that connects, on one end, Mission Street and the historic postal lobby with, on the other end, the outdoor gardens and residential towers. A fully sky-lit ceiling was installed over the gallery to allow the changes in weather and natural light to affect the qualities of the interior environment. Designed and installed by Doug Hollis, a major art fountain hushes the chatter of hundreds of visitors with the sound of falling droplets of water.

If Rincon Center is a classic case of civic space in a historic city like San Francisco, then the Queensway Bay Parking Structure is an archetypal public space for Southern California. It is located near the water in Long Beach across from the new Aquarium and a marine retail village, where virtually all visitors arrive by car. The portal into this series of public spaces at the water's edge is, in fact, a parking garage. Large by nature and six stories above grade, the mass of the building stands well above the elevation of the flat landfill site. Wall surfaces become signboards, stair columns act as vertical way-finding devices, and auto entrances are the real portals for most visitors to this seaside village.

Soon thereafter we initiated a relationship with the State of California when we were brought in to adapt the historic Broadway Department Store for a consolidation of State offices in the Los Angeles region. Governor Wilson had initiated a state-wide plan to bring together all office space scattered around each metropolitan region and relocate it in inner cities, in historic properties whenever possible. This was a move toward fiscal savings as well as an audacious urban policy in a largely suburban state by bringing employees into the city centers, re-using historic buildings, and enlivening urban neighborhoods and the small businesses that are located there.

The Junipero Serra State Office Building was one part preservation of the building exterior, one part design of the public interiors, and one part interior design of all the tenant space above grade. The ground floor was perhaps the most challenging element as we worked to unify the building's historic exterior with a contemporary interior, while integrating a broad program of public art throughout these spaces.

At the time of this work, the State was promoting an approach to public art referred to as Art in Architecture, wherein artists were called upon to participate in the fabric of the building, integrating their works into the actual architectural materials. Tony Berlant created lively and highly narrative covers for columns outside the central hearing room. A selection of local artists engraved elevator doors with drawings, turning the vestibules into panelized galleries. Poets and writers engraved their reflections on California into the limestone walls of the entry hall.

Following the Los Angeles work, we were commissioned to design the Capitol Area East End Complex: five buildings composed of offices for the State Departments of Education, Health and Human Services, and General Services. Comprising a million-and-a-half square feet of office space plus support and amenities, the mid-rise buildings cover the majority of five city blocks. The work at the State Capitol is widely seen as a successful public act, a new and improved workplace for thousands of State employees, and a celebrated effort on the part of California to require strong action in developing and designing highly sustainable buildings.

All five buildings stand at the eastern end of Capitol Park, on axis with the State Capitol Building. We designed arcades along the street side of all buildings to connect the park to the edges of our sites. Ground-level uses are publicly accessible wherever possible and lobbies are located as large embedded ovals with arched windows looking back to the State Capitol. Working with the art advisor Tamara Thomas, nearly 25 California artists were selected to create and locate artwork throughout

the multi-building complex. Exterior walls, floor patterns, gardens, chandeliers, statuary, engravings, and supergraphics all permeate the accessible ground level.

Great effort went into achieving high levels of sustainability for all buildings. Particular attention was given to limiting landfill waste, reducing fossil fuel-based energy consumption, and regulating indoor air quality. Strategies were established from the outset to recycle demolition materials and construction waste. Construction materials were locally sourced whenever possible, and recycled content was identified for exterior and interior building materials. Expended coal fly-ash was used in all concrete, structural steel employed recycled content, and interior ground floors incorporated recycled white marble removed from older State buildings. Native plant materials were selected for all landscape, and irrigated only as necessary from low-flow systems. High-performance shaded glass was employed in all upper floor offices while interior lighting systems included low-level ambient fixtures modulated by natural light levels and tied to motion detectors. Interior finish materials were selected based on natural and recycled content as well as indoor air quality. Underfloor power, telecommunications, and air delivery systems were installed to economize on service and maximize comfort. Upon completion, all buildings were LEED rated, exceeding California's Title 24 Energy Code by more than 25 percent. The Department of Education Building received a Gold LEED rating and was later upgraded to Platinum.

Following our work in Sacramento, which spanned some five years of design and construction, Solano

51

52   53

County commissioned us to design its new Government Center in downtown Fairfield, the county seat for one of California's fastest growing counties. Situated midway between San Francisco and Sacramento, the County provides housing and services in California's rural Central Valley to families who are frequently employed in either the Bay Area or the State Capitol. Again, like our work at the East End, Solano had a scattered Government Center without a central focus. We were commissioned to design a central structure that would house all County offices, a ground-level public hearing room for County Supervisors, and a major indoor atrium where county residents could convene and celebrate local events. Similarly, important outdoor landscapes were created, public art was introduced throughout the property, and a wide range of sustainability strategies led to a LEED Silver rating for the completed project.

The location of the project at the center of Main Street in historic Fairfield was a key decision on the part of the County. Re-inserting employees and visitors into the center of what was once a modest farming town held the promise of re-invigorating cultural and commercial life on a street that was widely abandoned when the interstate freeway system was put in place, bypassing dozens of formerly thriving small towns. At the front of the Government Center, we designed a large public plaza with seating, shade, water, large expanses for outdoor events, and a regularly scheduled farmers' market.

In 2008 we were invited to a competition for a new City Hall for Newport Beach, California. We were joined by the landscape architects, Olin Partners, and worked together to design a largely submerged set of buildings that would allow native parkland and trails to flow over the top of the structures, naturally insulating them and protecting established view corridors of the Pacific Ocean from nearby residential neighborhoods. In this community known for temperate weather, coastal recreation, and an informal lifestyle, our goal was to seamlessly integrate nature, recreation space, open civic space, Administrative Building, City Council chambers, and the existing Public Library.

In urban America, sports is one of the great themes of civic life. The owners of the Los Angeles Dodgers, the McCourt family, asked us recently to lead a team of design consultants in a major improvement plan for Dodger Stadium, which was opened in 1962 by then-team owner Walter O'Malley. The McCourts are looking ahead to the Stadium's 50th anniversary in 2012 and beyond, and preparing a plan for The Next 50. In the era when Dodger Stadium was built, the car was king and it ensured freedom and a kind of private territory affecting all buildings it served. At the opening of Dodger Stadium, fans could drive up to the perimeter of the structure, park in an assigned space, and walk directly into their section of the 56,000-seat venue. Because the site slopes 120 feet from the highest seats behind home plate to the outfield, reserved parking spaces circle the perimeter of the stadium such that a fan's car can be located near the level of his/her seat, bypassing all other levels. Efficiency from car to seat has reigned supreme. While other baseball clubs demolished their historic ballparks over the years, Dodger Stadium, once the most modern of stadiums, became the third oldest ballpark in the country. The McCourts

54

55

recognized the need to create improvements and expand amenities, yet they acknowledged the historic attraction of the original structure among fans, city dwellers, and preservationists alike. The decision was made to restore and reactivate Dodger Stadium as the icon it has become, and expand the perimeter into what the design team calls "The Green Necklace."

The perimeter of cars is proposed to be moved back from all sides of the Stadium by hundreds of feet allowing a new ring of gardens, more efficient parking, event spaces, and amenities to surround the historic building. Multiple gates will be established while a new main entry will be designed behind the outfield at the level of the playing field. Interior stadium concourses will no longer dead-end at right and left fields, but complete a circle behind the outfield bleachers at a new Dodger Plaza. The Plaza will be the center of a new Sports Museum, additional retail, and amenities, with office space at upper levels. What has been discovered is the possibility of increased socialization in these public/private spaces. In a city that is woefully short on evenly distributed public open space, private projects of scale are experimenting with the prospects for providing civic space. These private projects often attempt to base their new open space on historic models of civic space, and too often fail by trumping the goals of the public forum with the goals of the private marketplace. Yet, the human desire to congregate, socialize, and civilize seems irrepressible. Promise, in a city with so few public venues, appears to lie in a partnership of enlightened private entrepreneurship and public interest. These partnerships will continue to be crafted in the years to come.

At Johnson Fain, architecture is considered a unique outgrowth of culture. Responding to a sense of current critical issues, design looks outwardly to place, program, inhabitants' needs and technology for the cues from which compelling form is created. As a result, a priori design formulations are eschewed. We believe that design work, much like fine art, must be grounded in the realities of its own time and stretch to anticipate the future. As the firm frequently designs urban projects of scale, we believe that these projects, whether publicly or privately sponsored, must acknowledge their essential public status and serve the long-term needs of an ever-evolving and increasingly interdependent population. Thus, issues of sustainability, accessibility, and social equity are central for us.

Design in all disciplines tends toward form. The creation of an architectural icon is both a condensation of ideas as well as an expanding framework for the participation of present and future stakeholders. The principal dialectic of our time then, and the problem of the operation of design, is to recognize legitimate forces acting upon a condition, mapping them with precision and inclusivity, and then to direct patterns of physical intervention toward the becoming of architectural form. Umberto Eco has metaphorically described such an architecture, referring to "the open work" as "those creations that allow completion by the viewer, those that elicit multiple interpretations along coherent but uncharted lines." Such an architecture, we believe, can describe a vision of place, community and the future.

— Scott Johnson

56

57

58

Selected Works

Tall Buildings + Urban Habitats

MGM TOWER

MGM Tower was designed for Chicago-based JMB Realty Corp., and completed in 2003. The 704,000-square-foot, Class A office building was the first major high-rise structure to be constructed in Los Angeles in more than a decade. To best suit the needs of its high-profile tenants, Johnson Fain configured MGM Tower with large, flexible floor plates, dramatic glass corners, and long elevations to take advantage of the views in all directions. This arrangement maximizes the perimeter, allowing for more exterior offices with direct sunlight and skyline views.

The 35-story building contains expanded floor plates of 25,000 square feet on the lower floors, while upper floors consist of smaller floors for smaller tenants. The dramatically curved window wall encloses triangular glass corners highlighted by a richly detailed façade of glass and granite. Situated on six acres at the corner of Constellation Boulevard and Century Park West, MGM Tower enjoys a highly visible, prominent position at the western edge of Century City, California. Retail, restaurants, entertainment, and hotels are all part of this vibrant mixed-use neighborhood. The project includes a six-story, stand-alone parking structure housing more than 2,800 cars, and a generous garden designed to accommodate a wide range of plantings and publicly accessible fine art.

Since the building's completion, additional green measures have been taken to lower its energy requirements and to improve its operating efficiency. With these measures, plus the installation of Los Angeles' largest solar panel array, MGM Tower has received LEED Silver certification from the US Green Building Council.

Opposite
Rear courtyard with parking

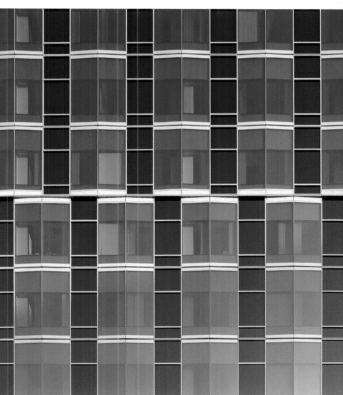

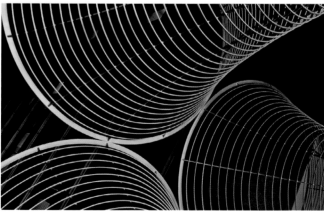

Lobby gallery to rear courtyard

METROPOLITAN LOFTS

Metropolitan Lofts is downtown Los Angeles' first new residential loft building. A mixed-use development of 264 loft-style apartments, the project includes amenities, ground-level live/work duplexes, and 11,000 square feet of retail space. Located in the South Park District of downtown Los Angeles, MetLofts is adjacent to LA Live! and Staples Center. A market-rate rental project with a 20 percent affordable housing component, MetLofts is the culmination of a redevelopment effort, led by the Community Redevelopment Authority, to turn a once-desolate city block of surface parking into a vibrant mixed-income residential community of affordable, senior, and family-oriented residences with flats and townhomes for the physically challenged.

The project features a generously landscaped courtyard with ground-level amenities visually open to other developments on the block and to pedestrians on 11th and Flower Streets. The lofts range in size from 690 to 1,400 square feet in one- and two-bedroom configurations. Also available are 11 street-level live/work units and studio apartments. Loft-like, each unit has large expanses of glass, high ceilings, open kitchens, and exposed structural and mechanical systems, with connectivity via high-speed internet. Amenities include a screening room, TV lounge, swimming pool, fitness center, and outdoor dining. A full building-height LED display is the result of the work of Electroland, digital artists who have created an interactive "welcome mat" at the entry to Metropolitan Lofts.

Interior courtyard

Intersection of residences and parking

Ground level social spaces

Opposite
Digital carpet and entrance

Top right
Residents' lounge

Bottom right
Ground level lobby

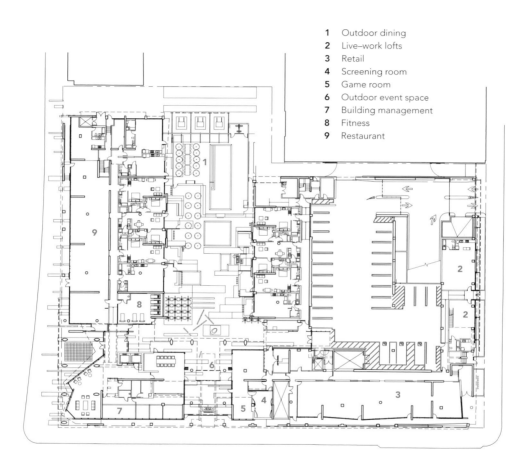

1 Outdoor dining
2 Live–work lofts
3 Retail
4 Screening room
5 Game room
6 Outdoor event space
7 Building management
8 Fitness
9 Restaurant

Ground level recreation center

Studio loft

Located in the heart of the Arts District at the gateway to downtown Dallas, Museum Tower is surrounded by distinguished architecture and public open space. Sited between the Morton H. Meyerson Symphony Center and the Nasher Sculpture Center, Museum Tower neighbors include the new Winspear Opera House, the Wyly Theatre, the historic Dallas Museum of Art, and the Booker T. Washington High School for the Performing and Visual Arts.

Museum Tower is a 42-story high-rise luxury condominium, providing 120 units in approximately 370,000 square feet, with below-grade parking. Individual residences are designed to take advantage of sweeping views of the city and beyond. An oval glass perimeter insures maximum natural light with private elevators directly serving each dwelling. Outdoor sky terraces are located at the ends of each floor, set deeply into the building to provide shade and sufficient space for furnishings and entertainment. Cultural amenities are available to residents at the ground floor including residents' lounge and library, art gallery, and meeting space. A Wellness Center including fitness, personal services, yoga, exhibition kitchen, dining, and swimming pool are located at the second level.

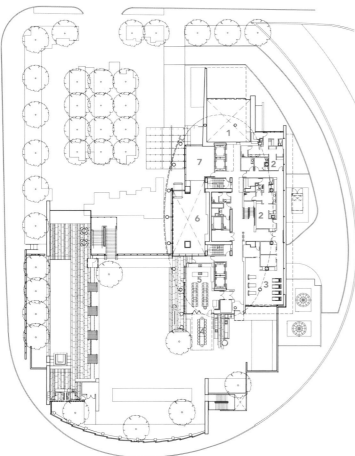

1 Art Gallery below
2 Dressing rooms
3 Fitness
4 Outdoor dining
5 Culinary center
6 Lobby below
7 Yoga studio

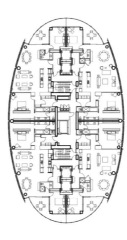

Residents' open kitchen and lounge

LEOPALACE 21

LeoPalace 21 is a new high-rise headquarters building designed for one of Japan's major homebuilding companies. The 35-story tower includes three lower levels of retail and banqueting space, 50,000 square feet of office space, 200 luxury hotel suites served from an express sky lobby, and 100 residential condominiums. The top floor is dedicated to a restaurant/bar with dramatic views of the city of Osaka. Intermediate viewing terraces and gardens punctuate the energy-efficient double skin of the tower. Tall, transparent, and highly sculptured, the building is faceted, reflecting sunlight by day and is illuminated at night.

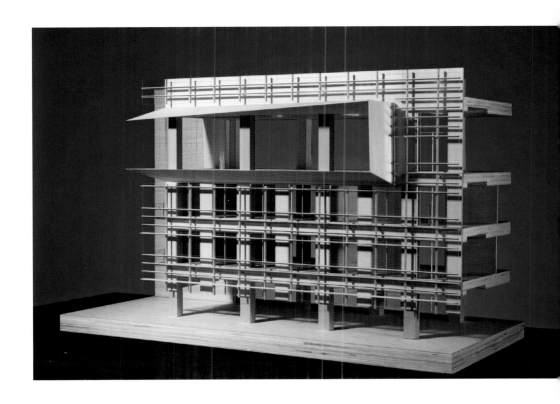

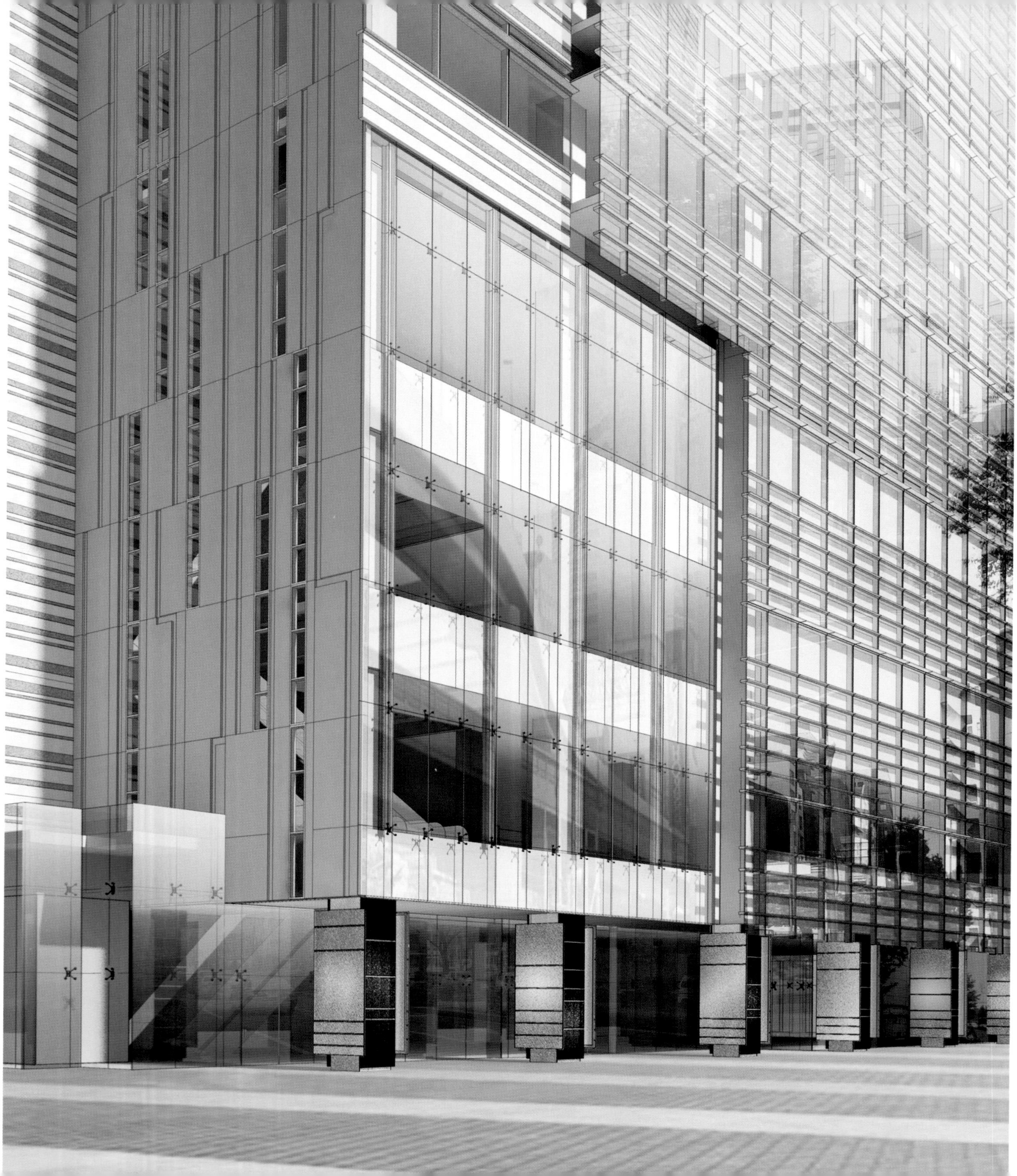

Opposite
Ground level entrance

Building entrance

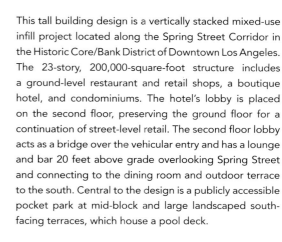

426 SOUTH SPRING

This tall building design is a vertically stacked mixed-use infill project located along the Spring Street Corridor in the Historic Core/Bank District of Downtown Los Angeles. The 23-story, 200,000-square-foot structure includes a ground-level restaurant and retail shops, a boutique hotel, and condominiums. The hotel's lobby is placed on the second floor, preserving the ground floor for a continuation of street-level retail. The second floor lobby acts as a bridge over the vehicular entry and has a lounge and bar 20 feet above grade overlooking Spring Street and connecting to the dining room and outdoor terrace to the south. Central to the design is a publicly accessible pocket park at mid-block and large landscaped south-facing terraces, which house a pool deck.

The tower's massing begins as a rectangular box at the street, encompassing the ground floor, the second floor, and parking to the top of the podium. Then, dramatically set back, the hotel floors rise and are sculpted in fractal patterns as they are transformed to residences above. The building's skin is a flush combination of concrete panels and glass windows of varying reflectivities. The tilted planes of the tower begin at the cornice level of adjacent historic buildings while the top breaks through the 150-foot district height limitation to capture views and establish a new scale in the neighborhood.

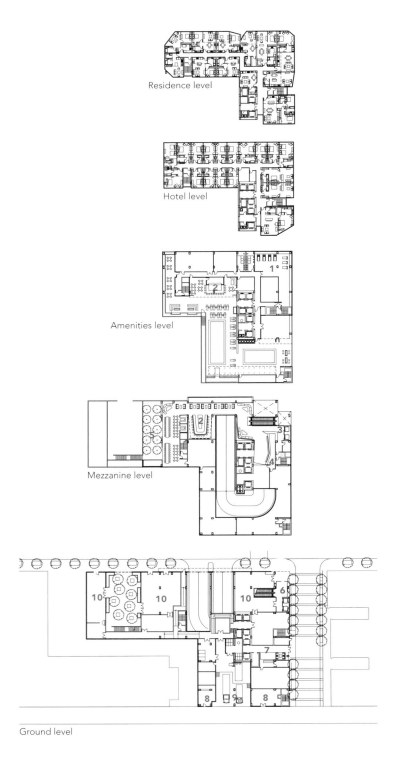

Residence level

Hotel level

Amenities level

Mezzanine level

Ground level

1   Fitness
2   Bar
3   Hotel lobby
4   Concierge
5   Terrace café
6   Hotel foyer
7   Residential lobby
8   Retail
9   Service
10   Restaurant

THE OFFICES OF JOHNSON FAIN

The offices of Johnson Fain are located in the historic Dominic Basso Chrysler DeSoto Showroom in Chinatown, in downtown Los Angeles. Located at 1201 North Broadway, the property is south of Elysian Park and near the site of the original Gaspar de Portolá encampment of 1781, which marked the beginning of the city's history as a pueblo at a bend in the Los Angeles River.

The neighborhood is currently undergoing a resurgence of activity with high-density housing projects, artists' studios and galleries, increased retail, loft conversions, and a new MTA Gold Line station. Across Broadway is the historic Cornfield site, soon destined to become a 32-acre State park.

The one-acre property includes the dealership building, which has been substantially renovated with reception, offices, meeting rooms, and high-bay loft space for the design studio. Architecture, urban design and planning, and interior design practices are co-mingled in two column-free vaulted spaces illuminated by north-facing skylights. Sunlight and natural ventilation systems have been reactivated to service the studio, the model fabrication shop, and the digital platform center, which networks all workstations and coordinates plotting, model prototyping, and 3D animation activities.

Studio entrance

Pastoral Landscapes

OPUS ONE WINERY

The Opus One Winery, a joint venture of the Robert Mondavi Winery and Baron Philippe de Rothschild, is a unique collaboration between a renowned California vintner and a celebrated European winemaker. The winery is set in 100 acres of vineyards in the heart of the Napa Valley, California's preeminent wine-growing region. The unique, 70,000-square-foot, low-profile structure is concealed from view by a crescent-shaped landscaped berm. The entry to the front of the winery bisects the berm and leads to a courtyard shaded by olive trees. The semicircular courtyard is surrounded by perimeter arcades that link public functions including spaces for reception, wine tasting, administrative offices, public relations, and kitchen facilities. The lower level is exclusively devoted to winemaking. The space beneath the berm shelters the Grand Chai where first-year barrels are on display, overlooked by the main tasting room. Other functions on this level include fermentation, barrel cleaning, barrel storage, bottling, and delivery.

The building plan and section are organized to encourage "gravity flow" of the winemaking process, whereby grapes are delivered to the winery high, then fermented and barreled low. This ensures that there is a minimum of mechanical movement and disturbance of the wine. Barrel room cooling is provided through a radiant system embedded within the concrete building structure. The primary exterior cladding is domestic limestone, weathered California redwood, natural oak, concrete floors, and stainless steel hardware and details. All interior design elements, including furnishings, carpets, and lighting fixtures, were designed and selected to expand the architectural vision of the building and to reflect a unity of winemaking, food, and artful living.

Opposite
First-year barrel cellar

Bottom left
Tasting room

Bottom right
Stairwell to basement cellar

BYRON WINERY

A sweeping, curved roof, reminiscent of the rolling hills surrounding the site, is the central feature of the Byron Winery. In keeping with California's experimental tradition, the 32,000-square-foot Byron Winery is both strikingly futuristic and respectful of the land from which it grows. Built from natural materials, the winery is formed of cedar planks, steel windows, and zinc sheet roofing. Highlighted by free-form plaster panels of intense earth pigments, a long shaded portico runs the length of the building, providing entry to the tasting and barrel rooms and a panoramic view of the vineyards below.

The project's technical features include 10,000 square feet of barrel aging facilities, with a cave-like environment for optimal humidity and temperature control, gravity-flow design, state-of-the-art technology including specially designed grape sorting tables, and portable tank transport systems. A tasting room, catering kitchen, and wine library are also included. The winery is situated on 640 acres of vineyards and has an annual production capacity of 70,000 cases.

Tasting room

View from exterior through tasting room to barrel and tank rooms beyond

THE CLUBHOUSE AT SANDY LANE RESORT

The Clubhouse at Sandy Lane Resort encompasses 55,000 square feet of hospitality space and is located on a hillside overlooking golf and the west coast of Barbados. Arrival to the building is from a large cobbled motor court surrounded by a garden arcade. The entry is located in a tall conical vestibule, which recalls historic sugar mills from the island's agricultural past. The building's exterior is dressed in bands of coral plaster and sanded Portuguese limestone. Primary lounges and the principal restaurant and bar are shaded by a deep radial soffit that protects guests and golfers from the hot tropical sun, and allows the building to ventilate naturally by virtue of the frequent trade winds. Views to the Sandy Lane and Green Monkey golf courses, both designed by Tom Fazio, and to the coastline beyond are wide and unobstructed.

Both the Golf Pro Shop and the Member's Lounge are designed as circular forms to maximize broad views of the tropical landscape. Administration space and the men's and women's locker rooms are rectangular in form, flank the public space, and help to form the arcaded motor court. The golf cart maintenance and barn, as well as employee facilities, storage, and support spaces, are on the basement floor. Interior finishes in the public areas include hand-troweled coral, cement plasters, marble, and limestone, and interior millwork is executed in dark farmed mahogany. The floors are designed with two shades of honed travertine in large geometric patterns that extend out into the landscape.

Above left
Dressing room
Above right
Golf pro shop
Left
Locker room lounge

AETNA SPRINGS CLUBHOUSE AND RESORT

Johnson Fain was commissioned to provide visioning and architectural design services to restore the historic Aetna Springs as a premier resort. The new 8,800-square-foot golf clubhouse recalls the quintessential North Bay style, relying heavily on wood construction that reflects the highly detailed craftsmanship of the late 19th century. The clubhouse offers state-of-the-art amenities while preserving the character of the legendary resort and bygone era. Taking cues from the Bernard Maybeck-designed dining hall, the clubhouse features large exposed wood trusses, stone columns, fireplaces, and generously scaled chandeliers. The sweeping verandas and expansive glass walls provide natural light and panoramic views of the historic, restored course and the rolling hills surrounding the Pope Valley. Inventive details and a rich array of materials provide the clubhouse with a distinctive and consistent character.

The clubhouse's materials, structure and siting celebrate the historic golf course and the area's tranquility and natural beauty. Working with Johnson Fain, noted golf course designer Tom Doak meticulously restored the original nine-hole course, the oldest on the West Coast. The two-story clubhouse contains a main dining hall, lounge, bar, pro shop, and locker rooms, and is the social center of this restored resort community.

AMERICAN INDIAN CULTURAL CENTER AND MUSEUM

Since 1996, Johnson Fain has worked with the Native American Cultural and Educational Authority of the State of Oklahoma to plan and design the American Indian Cultural Center and Museum. The mission of the complex is the study, production, and celebration of all aspects of Native American culture on a 330-acre site located on the Canadian River, south of downtown Oklahoma City. The genesis of the physical design of the project grew out of Native American spiritual concepts and the desire to achieve a seamless relationship between the earth and building.

Site development and landscape design express landscape patterns of Native American habitation and culture, as well as exhibition and activity programs through form. Themes include "encampment," and the "three ecologies": the woodlands, the river, and the plains, which are woven into the site plan. The building's design draws upon the use of monumental natural materials such as earth, timber, natural stone, and Corten steel.

Architectural space in the project is created to underscore the four elements recurrent in Native American tribal belief systems: earth, fire, air, and water. The promontory berm is built of earth, a campfire resides in the heart of the complex, windpipes acknowledge the movement of air in the Courtyard of the Nations, and water is omnipresent in both the nearby river and at the entrance. The project includes a ceremonial Hall of the People with exhibition galleries, assembly, and a discovery center for hands-on educational activities and research.

Master site plan

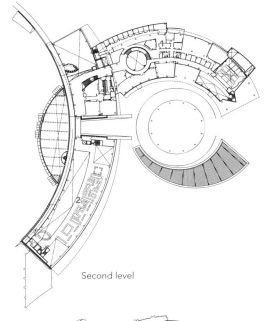

Second level

1   Offices and media lab
2   Mezzanine gallery
3   North gallery
4   Gift shop
5   Discovery center
6   Artist's studio
7   Theater
8   Visitor center
9   South gallery
10   Hall of the people

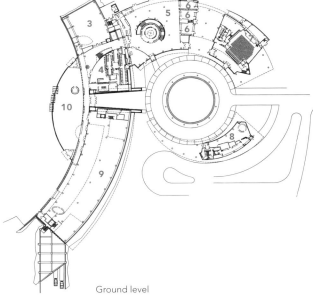

Ground level

Left and below
Visitor center

Technology, Education + Research

AMGEN CENTER

Amgen, Inc. is the world's largest biotechnology company. Johnson Fain has provided comprehensive design services at Amgen Center since 1995. Almost 20 years ago, Amgen began as a corporate start-up in a single building in Thousand Oaks, California. As the company grew, it acquired adjoining properties as they became available until the present 130-acre site was fully assembled. Establishing a master plan concept that accommodates expansion of new buildings and re-works open spaces, pedestrian and automobile circulation, and new employee amenities, Johnson Fain has worked to transform a formerly industrial neighborhood into a friendly, landscaped, and well-organized environment.

The designs of many major buildings on the campus have been commissioned. These include offices, laboratories, parking structures, a fitness center, and executive conference centers. Johnson Fain has provided interior design services for most of these buildings. Incorporating new concepts of natural daylighting, interactive teaming, efficient space plans, and comfortable workflow for employees, the interior designs have established standards for an evolving and productive workplace for Amgen employees. Johnson Fain continues to assist Amgen with its continued growth.

Opposite
Headquarters buildings with landscape

Pergola

Central paseo

GENENTECH HEADQUARTERS

Genentech, headquartered in South San Francisco, is a world leader in biotechnology. Johnson Fain has provided a wide range of design services for Genentech including campus planning, architecture, and interior design. At the heart of its campus is a new master planned administrative office complex. This design-built complex, located on a bluff overlooking the San Francisco Bay, consists of three five-story office buildings clustered around a circular courtyard. The ground floor contains common facilities for the employees such as a cafeteria, Genen Store, and conference/meeting rooms.

The treatment of the building façades, using natural, sustainable, and durable materials, reflects the activities within. Private offices on the upper floors take advantage of the extraordinary outward views of the Bay while common space and conferencing look to the landscaped courtyard within the site. With the integration of natural flagstone in paving and ground level walls and columns, the building finishes create a harmonious relationship with the drought-tolerant Northern California landscaping on the site.

THE HORIZON

Johnson Fain was commissioned by Lincoln Property Company to design the first new commercial office development in Playa Vista, California, the former home of the Howard Hughes Aircraft Company. The six-acre campus features 950,000 square feet of Class A office space and sets the standard for future projects in the region. The new building design represents the convergence of a state-of-the-art workplace environment and a continuation of the industrial character of the surrounding historic Hughes buildings. Bold in scale and designed to the edge of their sites, the buildings are configured to mimic the flat, flush metal walls of the original buildings while providing flexible, uninterrupted floorplans required by technology, media, and other high-profile creative tenants.

Building materials, textures, and finishes take their cues from both historic and state-of-the-art industrial applications including zinc-finished corrugated sheet steel, and aluminum unitized window systems with projecting sunshades, sills, and high-performance glass. Silk-screened laminated glass transoms, perforated corrugated panels, and sunshades assist in maximizing daylight and views while limiting heat and energy consumption. The buildings respond to solar orientation through a differentiation of building elevations. Informal outdoor plazas and recreational areas have been designed with native plant species characteristic of Southern California beach regions.

CAL(IT)^2

The California Institute for Telecommunications and Information Technology Cal(IT)^2 is a new high-technology research and development facility at the University of California, Irvine. The project is one of the California Institutes for Science and Innovation initiated and funded by the California Governor's Office. The new building provides a physical platform for a wide range of multidisciplinary projects and programs for the School of Engineering, the Office of Academic Computing, Environmental Science, and Media Arts, and the School of Education. Cal(IT)^2 supports these programs' research in information technology and innovative uses of digital media.

Comprising 120,000 square feet and four stories, the building includes a combination of clean rooms for silicon chip-based manufacturing processes, wet and dry laboratories, classrooms, offices, and meeting facilities. Also included are rooms for experimental media and a gallery for the display and demonstration of experiments in new media and technology. The building is composed of two major wings, one for research space, and the other for a 100-seat multimedia lecture theater, media center, and Institute offices.

Opposite
Multipurpose atrium

Top
Clean room

Bottom
Lecture hall

SUTARDJA DAI HALL

The newest research facility on the University of California, Berkeley campus is another project initiated by the Center for Information Technology Research in the Interest of Society (CITRIS), and is planned to fuel economic growth through technology research and manufacturing. Designed to turn research into socially useful commercial applications, the $127-million facility includes classrooms and laboratories, plus a 149-seat auditorium, cybercafé, technology museum, distance-learning classrooms, and Marvell Nanofabrication Laboratory, whose two large clean rooms are equipped with some of the world's most advanced semiconductor-fabrication equipment.

Recently renamed Sutardja Dai Hall, it is now the new home of CITRIS and the Banatao Institute@CITRIS Berkeley. CITRIS is a multi-disciplinary program that combines the skills and talents of more than 300 faculty researchers and thousands of students from four UC campuses—Berkeley, Davis, Merced, and Santa Cruz—with industrial partners from more than 60 corporations. As the headquarters for CITRIS, the 141,000-square-foot building is open to researchers from the four UC campuses in wide-ranging disciplines, including engineering, energy, health, law, public policy, political science, and new media. The new building replaces Davis Hall North in the northeast corner of the UC Berkeley campus and consists of five above-ground and two basement floors. The new building is located within the College of Engineering quadrant. The design, massing, and scale of the building respond to the nearby Arts & Crafts buildings as well as the adjacent Naval Architecture Building.

The largest new high school for the Los Angeles Unified School District, Miguel Contreras Learning Complex is located on approximately 18 acres in the Crown Hill District of downtown Los Angeles. The project addresses critical overcrowding at nearby schools by providing 71 classrooms and major athletic facilities shared with other schools in the District. Facilities that can be shared with the community at large, such as the auditorium, are located at one end of the site to avoid disruption to classes at the other end. Reflecting the density and scale of its urban location, the high school accommodates approximately 1,900 students in 221,100 square feet of space and comprises an auditorium/ administration building, two classroom wings, library/ multimedia labs, food services/cafeteria, two gymnasia, and a parking structure.

The classroom wings are distinctive with their open-air, vertical circulation stairs, open-air corridors, and floating corrugated steel roof located above the circulation spine to provide protection from the inclement weather and encourage natural ventilation. The courtyard is enlivened with distinctive smaller garden elements and performance spaces, each being extensions of ground-level teaching rooms. These include an outdoor music garden adjacent to the instrumental music classroom, an outdoor stage platform adjacent to the dance classroom, an herb garden and informal "cook out" pergola adjacent to the culinary arts classroom, and a stepped garden for nature sketching adjacent to the art studio. Garden steps on the western edge of the courtyard function as an informal amphitheater for school announcements. The two gymnasia, sports fields, olympic-size swimming pool, and parking are located in the northern portion of the site reached by a pedestrian bridge.

Student and faculty dining center

Pedestrian bridge

Left
Third floor academic wing

Below left
Development at the edge of downtown
Los Angeles

Right
Men's and women's gymnasia

1 Athletic fields
2 Swimming pool
3 Classrooms
4 Library / media center
5 Cafeteria
6 Auditorium
7 Administration
8 Gymnasium
9 Locker rooms / athletic offices

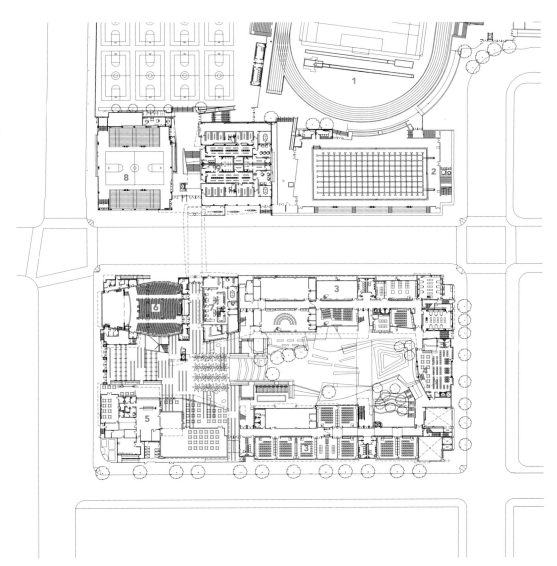

ROY ROMER MIDDLE SCHOOL

The Roy Romer Middle School is located at the northwest corner of Laurel Canyon Boulevard and Hamlin Street in North Hollywood, California. The site's context includes the 170 Freeway located a quarter-mile west of the site, and air traffic from nearby Van Nuys and Burbank Airports. The nine-and-a-half-acre, L-shaped site is bounded by single-family residences to the west, Laurel Canyon Boulevard to the east, and Kittridge and Hamlin Streets on the north and south respectively.

The new Middle School accommodates 1,600 students in 160,000 square feet of enclosed space. Campus buildings are organized around a large public square that serves as the school's entry and major social center. Accessed from Laurel Canyon Boulevard, the square is defined by a 97,000-square-foot classroom and administration wing to the north and, paralleling Laurel Canyon Boulevard, a 25,000-square-foot, two-story multipurpose building along the south and a two-story 6,000-square-foot multimedia center at the northwest corner. A fourth, 19,000-square-foot gymnasium building is located between the parking area and the playing field that extends from the plaza at the east to the westerly border of the site. The organizational concept for the project is based on a series of north–south buildings and landscape zones that create privacy and a variety of intimate spaces for small group social activity and instruction.

Central courtyard looking into academic wing

Front elevation

Multipurpose student center

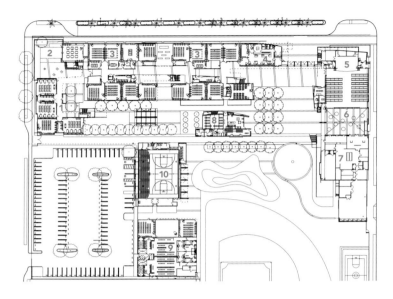

1 Science center
2 Arts courtyard
3 Classrooms
4 Administration offices
5 Multipurpose theater
6 Dining
7 Cafeteria and kitchen
8 Library / media center
9 Locker rooms
10 Gymnasium

Outdoor dining

Lecture hall

Houses

This 4,200-square-foot single-story home is located in the Napa Valley. The house sits on the upper portion of a 42-acre site accessed by a private road with a vineyard at the lower end of the site. The house has been designed as a weekend home and office for a couple, as well as a place for entertaining and overseeing a new winery venture. The design concept is a highly ordered series of rectilinear volumes clad in precisely finished steel panels. The house is designed to be an integrated part of its natural surroundings, with elements such as a central living space composed of glass walls that provide a uniquely framed view out to the landscape, and slender steel columns and concrete piers that support exposed wood soffits and mirror the many existing trees on the site.

The interior material palette ranges from simple plywood ceilings and polished concrete floors to the rich texture of cleft quartzite stone stairs and Mexican glass mosaic tiled floors and walls. Interior walls are veneered in plaster in subtle colors. Living spaces are further defined by maple-veneered ceilings that are suspended beneath exposed wooden roof joists. Millwork elements are custom-designed and composed of ebonized and stained maple veneers, brushed stainless steel, and silver travertine. The landscape design includes stepped terraces, a lap pool, spa, barbecue, and an exterior fireplace set within the natural landscape of boulders and native oak trees.

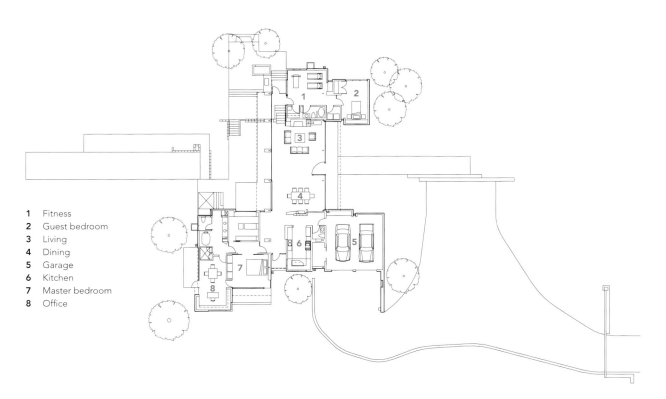

1 Fitness
2 Guest bedroom
3 Living
4 Dining
5 Garage
6 Kitchen
7 Master bedroom
8 Office

View to vineyard and Napa Valley beyond

This house on White Sulphur Springs Road is six miles west of Main Street in Saint Helena, California, in the heart of the Napa Valley. Located 500 feet above the valley floor, the house sits on 60 acres of wilderness bordering California State parkland and Iron Mine Creek. The house is sited immediately above a hillside vineyard on a long, narrow spit of land, which is accessed from the west and looks out over a small vineyard eastward to the valley. The driveway is located in a grove of native oaks, and the entrance to the house is marked by a 200-foot-long uninterrupted wall bisecting the house beyond.

Beginning at the driveway, the wall passes through the entrance, and down into a central gallery, culminating in a living room defined by three walls of glass and two flanking fireplaces. Circulation throughout the house is defined by a series of stone steps and landings that follow the descent of the hill and form the basis of the plan. Over the length of the house, four glazed thresholds separate the longitudinal procession of the building with bands of glass at walls and ceiling, giving slivered views of the landscape left and right. This long wall further defines the house by separating private spaces (bedroom and baths) and communal spaces (gallery, kitchen, dining, studio, and living area).

Finishes in the house are elemental: sandblasted plywood panels, plastered white walls, rough-sawn cedar doors and walls, and steel window frames and millwork crafted in domestic quarter-sawn ash.

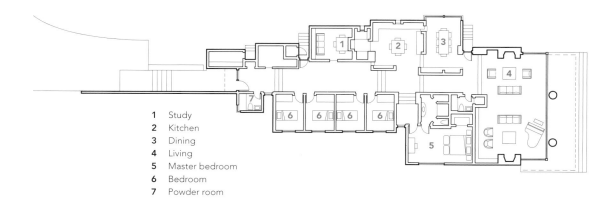

1 Study
2 Kitchen
3 Dining
4 Living
5 Master bedroom
6 Bedroom
7 Powder room

Entrance

Living room

Entry vestibule to master bedroom

Dining room millwork

MALIBU HOUSE

This house was designed for a family of five and is located on a site overlooking the Pacific Ocean in Malibu, California. The project includes a two-story, 8,000-square-foot addition to an existing two-story, 4,000-square-foot structure. The plan of the house is configured to be linear in an attempt to provide shared views from a wide range of rooms. The façades and fenestration are a direct response to the axial views from within the house to the coastline below and beyond.

The central feature of the house is a double-story rotunda, which encloses the living room with a 22-foot tall glass wall overlooking the ocean, and encases a radial staircase that connects both floors. Entry to the house is from a motor court at the upper floor. Bedrooms are located at this level with higher views, while living and social spaces are below, extending out to the pool deck, garden, and vineyards at the rear of the site.

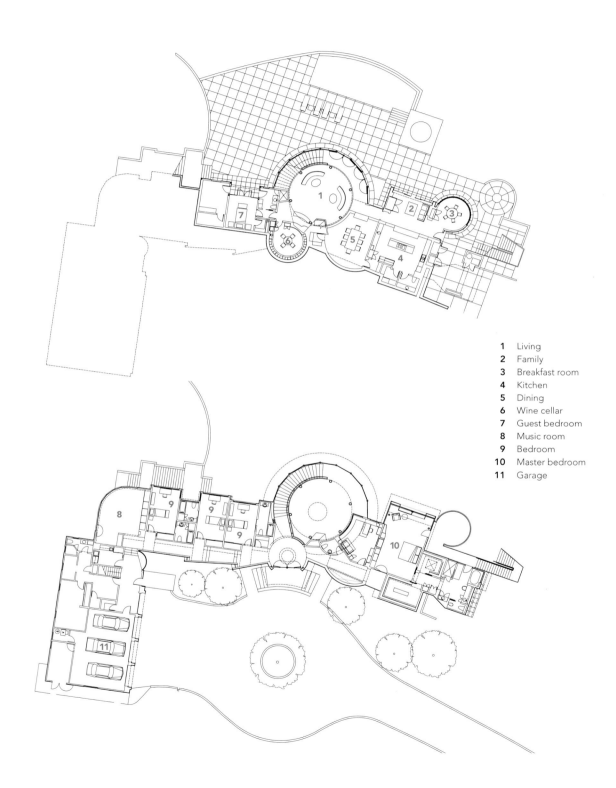

1 Living
2 Family
3 Breakfast room
4 Kitchen
5 Dining
6 Wine cellar
7 Guest bedroom
8 Music room
9 Bedroom
10 Master bedroom
11 Garage

Living room with entrance above

Library over dining room

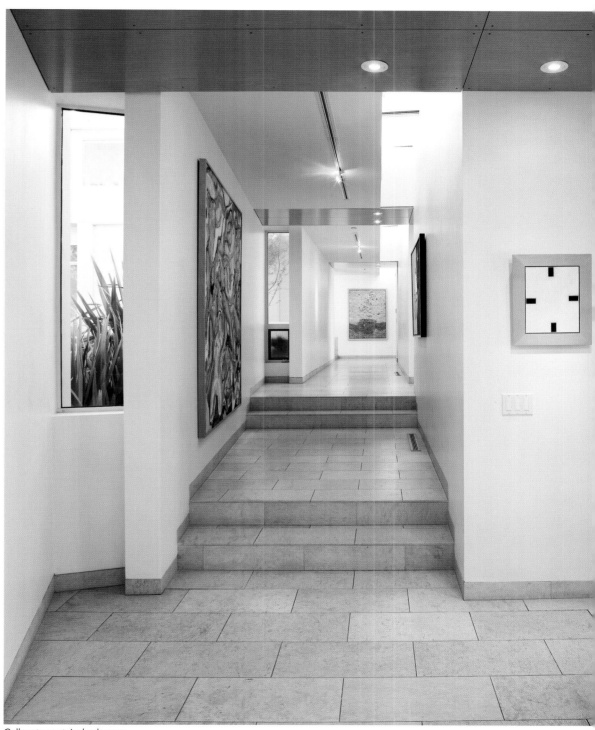

Gallery to upstairs bedrooms

Master bedroom

LOS ALTOS HILLS HOUSE

This 6,800-square-foot, single-story home is located at the southern end of the San Francisco Bay on a 12-acre hilltop site. The project represents a substantial expansion and remodel of an important modern house designed in the mid-1950s by John Funk and featured in Sally Woodbridge's seminal book, *Bay Area Houses*. The house had been vandalized prior to its acquisition and had fallen into disrepair.

The design preserves all primary steel structure and window frames, the principal ceiling plane, and the original radiant concrete floor slab, which runs throughout the original house. The building was expanded to accommodate the activities of a young and growing family of five. Accordingly, kitchen and dining spaces were enlarged at the perimeter of the building envelope where natural daylight could be maximized.

Deep overhangs protect expansive glass walls from solar heat gain while large operable panes allow ample cross ventilation to provide a complete passive cooling system. New skylight monitors in the roof provide natural light to the interior core of the house. Play rooms and study spaces have been introduced at both ends of the house to allow parental supervision and proximity to young children. The original bedroom wing was expanded to include interior wardrobe and storage as well as expanded bath and dressing areas.

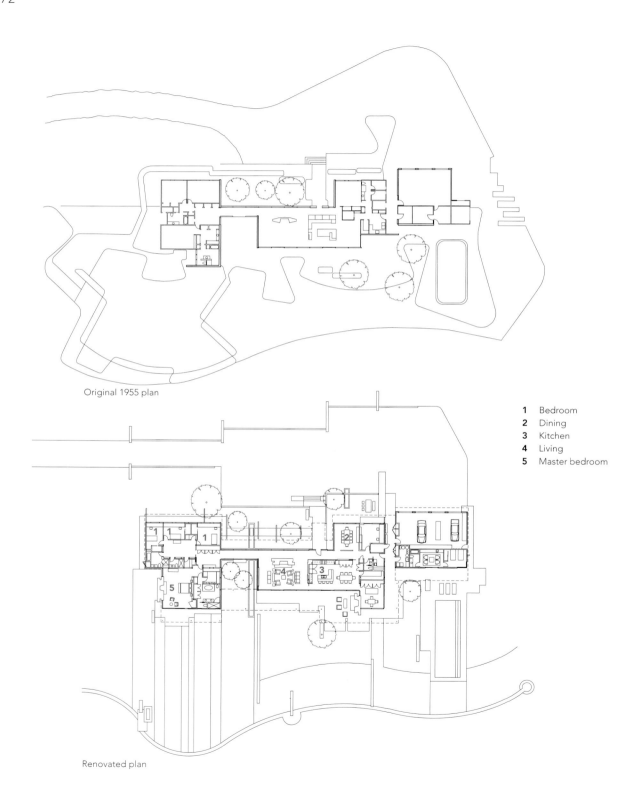

Original 1955 plan

Renovated plan

1 Bedroom
2 Dining
3 Kitchen
4 Living
5 Master bedroom

Above left
Living room

Left
Dine-in kitchen

Master bedroom

Master bathroom

LARCHMONT VILLAGE TOWNHOUSE

This three-story, 5,000-square-foot urban townhouse is built on a commercial street in central Los Angeles. The client and family wished to live within walking distance of commercial services in a mixed-use urban environment, and reduce automobile dependence. The exterior façade is composed of corrugated steel panels and custom glass curtain wall. Precision has been achieved through the manipulation of these two material systems into pure geometric forms, which express the inner workings of the house, and avoid the formal language of the traditional single-family dwelling.

The ground floor provides space for laundry, housekeeping, utilities, and a large room facing the garden used by the children as a studio and electronic music room. Shelter for automobiles is under the elevated slab of the second floor. Compact urban gardens exist on three sides of the house: flower and kitchen garden to the rear, outdoor room with canopy trees and hedgerow wall to the front, and winter vegetable garden to the south. The second floor is the primary activity floor, with living and dining rooms, kitchen, private patio, swimming pool, and the master bedroom suite. The third floor includes a library and children's bedrooms. With the exception of individual bedrooms, all rooms interconnect horizontally and vertically, opening up the house and maximizing common space.

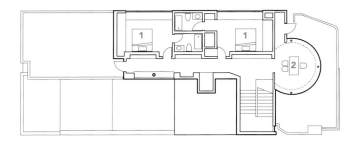

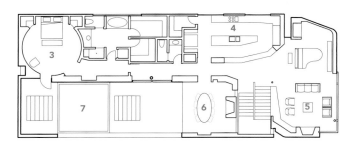

1 Bedroom
2 Study
3 Master bedroom
4 Kitchen
5 Living
6 Dining
7 Pool
8 Library
9 Housekeepers
10 Wine cellar

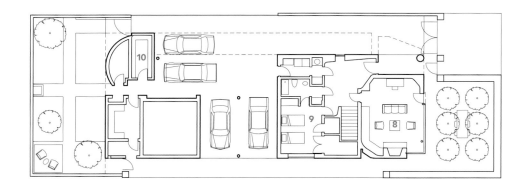

Second floor patio

Installations

Second floor

Master bedroom

Study

Civic Space

CAPITOL AREA EAST
END COMPLEX

Located at the easterly terminus of Capitol Park, this project is an ambitious multi-block mixed-use development that consolidates the headquarters operations of three major departments of California State government. Sixty-four hundred employees of the Departments of Health Services, Education, and General Services are housed in the five-building, 1.5-million-square-foot complex along with 1,500 parking spaces.

The California Department of Education Headquarters, Block 225, was the first of this five-building development to be completed. The project was delivered through a Bridged Design–Build process, with Johnson Fain acting as master design architect including planning and interior design. At 336,000 square feet and six stories high, Block 225 was the largest project in the world to receive a LEED 2.0 Gold rating upon completion, and has since been upgraded to Platinum status. The Department of Health Services and General Services are housed in the second portion of the Capitol Area East End Complex, which has received a LEED Silver rating.

Public amenities include retail, a community police station, a 300-seat auditorium, and a childcare center for up to 100 infants, toddlers, and pre-schoolers including outdoor play areas. Previously, employees were housed in more than 20 properties throughout the region. In consolidating staff into the new complex, the State has vacated rental space, increased employee productivity, and located 6,400 employees within walking distance of the central city, services, and major public transportation systems.

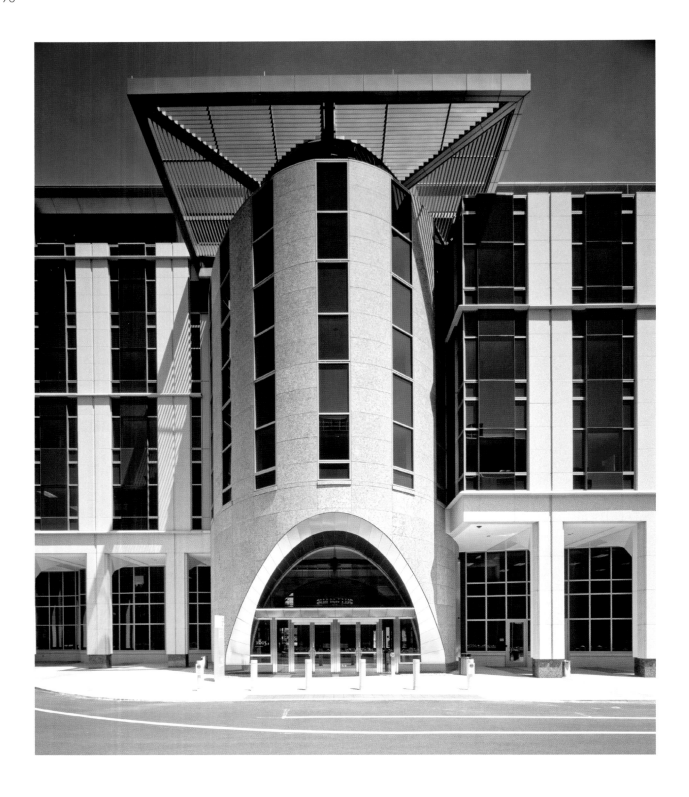

IT WAS THE SECRETS OF HEAVEN AND EARTH THAT I DESIRED TO LEARN.

MARY SHELLEY 1818

Central lobby, Department of Education building

300-seat auditorium

Ground floor elevator vestibule

SOLANO COUNTY
GOVERNMENT CENTER

Solano County, one of the fastest growing counties in the State of California, recently brought its many departments together under one roof as part of a comprehensive "smart-growth" consolidation effort. The project consists of a six-story, 300,000-square-foot administration building with a five-level, 1,008-space parking garage equipped with a large solar electric farm and electric vehicle stations, plus an adjacent two-story, 43,000-square-foot probation building and a 25,000-square-foot public plaza. The entire county campus stretches nearly three city blocks in downtown Fairfield and is located next to the County Courthouse and Justice Center, with all important governmental functions now adjacent to one another. The new administration building, the project's central structure, now houses more than 800 county employees, combining 16 departments from 15 different locations in two cities. The project embodies the smart-growth strategies of an infill development located within walking distance of Main Street and a multi-modal train station.

The six-story administration building, a LEED Silver project, incorporates many sustainable features, including the recycling of major building materials and a gray water recovery system. The building also exceeds California's Title 24 Energy Efficiency Standards by 10 percent, using high-efficiency HVAC systems, low ambient lighting systems, and a photovoltaic panel system for the conversion of solar energy. The principal project goal was to create a landmark community building at the historic center of Fairfield. The steel-framed, glass-sheathed building's iconic image is marked by a distinctive six-story inverted pyramid at the main entrance. The central lobby is double-height and anchored by a monumental staircase with broad landings, and incorporates publicly funded artwork. The generous central lobby serves as a public gathering space for exhibits, press conferences, and community events.

Above right
Ground level lobby and reception hall

Right
County boardroom

JUNIPERO SERRA STATE OFFICE BUILDING

The rehabilitation of the 533,000-square-foot, former Broadway Department Store was undertaken to convert the historic structure into a multi-departmental California State office building. As a historic landmark within the nationally registered Broadway Theater and Commercial District, the original design is typical of early 20th-century commercial architecture whereby a window system based on the Chicago School tradition was integrated into Italian Neoclassical architecture.

The building provides usable office space for ten departments of the State, plus ground-floor pedestrian-serving retail and two subterranean parking levels. More than 1,000 employees are housed in the refurbished structure. Interior components include private and open plan office space, multiple conference rooms, courtrooms, multi-purpose room, and ground-floor café. Terrazzo patterns, combined with flamed limestone walls and stainless steel accessories, create a modern and durable response to the historic building. A large public arts program has been integrated throughout the interior architecture of the project.

Elevator doors

Elevator vestibule with mosaic art

Ground floor lobby for the Central Hearing Room

The Newport Beach City Hall and Park site is central to major landmarks and destinations in Orange County. Easy access exists to the University of California, Irvine (a center of learning and new knowledge), Newport Center and the Irvine Spectrum (centers of commerce and industry), Fashion Island (a center of style and a model Southern California retail destination), and Newport Bay, the islands, the harbor, and beaches.

The site is characterized by a host of native coastal plants and a topography that provides uninterrupted views of the coast. A desire to preserve these views, maximize the native landscape, and respect mandated viewshed restrictions forms the basis of the design concept. Two central buildings, one for civic administration, the other to house the City Council chamber, are set into the ground, allowing the extraordinary public park to pass over the top of each building as lush planted roofs. A new major civic plaza creates a foreground for the two buildings with views to the surrounding community and the Pacific Ocean. Circulation in the park passes through the new City Hall complex and connects to the adjacent library building. The park, City Hall, and library are unified. Views to the surrounding landscape and the ocean beyond are maximized. Parking is conveniently located to serve all parts of the new project plus the library.

The park is organized around a half-mile boardwalk, which runs along the primary ridges of the site and connects major ecological and programmatic spaces. The boardwalk and City Hall terraces will be focal points for civic life, much as the Balboa Pavilion and Pier are icons of the city's recreational amenities.

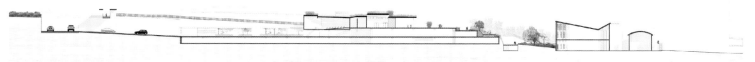

Site section

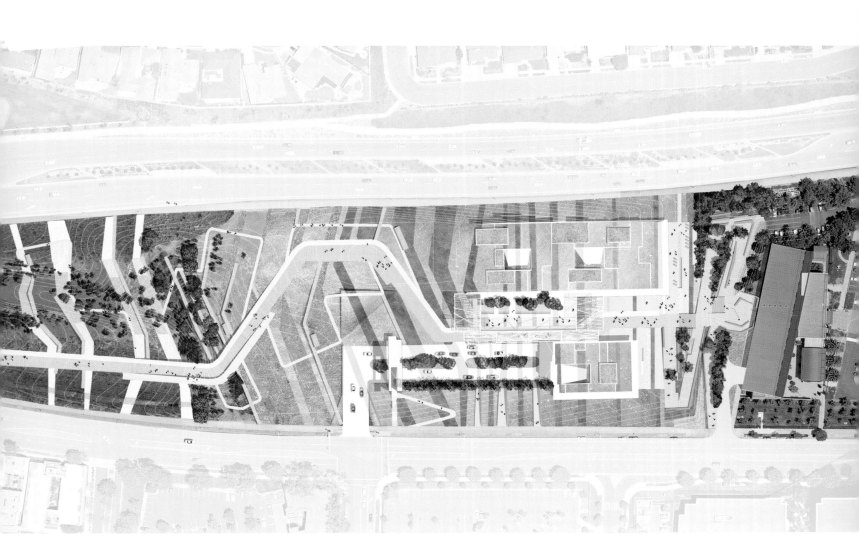

QUEENSWAY BAY PARKING STRUCTURE

This five-level parking structure, located on Shoreline Drive in Long Beach, California, provides 1,500 spaces for the Aquarium of the Pacific, an IMAX theater, and a variety of seaport shops, restaurants, and entertainment venues. The unique and inviting structure was designed to provide an entertaining gateway for visitors to Queensway Bay. The project's theme consists of a playful interpretation of various marine life, and features a "nautical" staircase, and a façade with the likeness of sea bubbles and ocean waves. Blue neon outlines aluminum panels that slope along one side of the building and give the appearance of a wave crashing onto Shoreline Drive. Matching the appearance of a ship's sails, the stair and elevator tower is 80 feet tall and functions as a landmark to sailors to find their way back to the Long Beach Marina.

Landscape design includes a centrally located fountain with three playful bronze dolphins. Careful consideration went into the selection of the sea lavender, Australian bluebells, morning glory, lily of the Nile, and pride of Madeira, used to accentuate the arbors. On the garage floor, schools of fish direct pedestrians to the elevators and stairs. A ramp separates pedestrians from vehicular traffic while each level of the structure has its own color scheme, incorporating imagery of the sea. Electric vehicles receive special accommodation and recharging.

Top
Façade detail

Bottom
Automobile entrance

Johnson Fain is leading a design team in creating a comprehensive stadium improvement plan for Dodger Stadium. The plan will bring the most up-to-date amenities to Los Angeles Dodger fans while preserving and celebrating the tradition of the historic venue first opened in 1962. The improvements, anticipated to be completed by opening day of the 2012 season, will set a new standard for Dodger Stadium as the home of Los Angeles baseball for the next 50 years. The new facilities are being designed to meet LEED Silver sustainability standards.

The Dodger Stadium NEXT 50 plan features Dodger Way, a ceremonial new gateway and urban plaza surrounded by an administrative office building for the Dodgers organization, the Dodger Experience Museum, an interactive venue showcasing the history of the Dodgers and baseball worldwide, a flagship Dodger Store, and the Dodger Cafe. Connecting all the elements of the project is the Green Necklace, a ring of gardens, open plazas, and amenities surrounding the existing stadium. The Top of the Park Plaza, located at the highest elevation on site, will feature 360-degree views encompassing the downtown skyline and Santa Monica Bay, the Hollywood Hills and San Gabriel Mountains, and the Dodger Stadium baseball diamond. Other features within the Green Necklace are a consolidation of parking into two nine-level structures, a range of food service and retail concessions, and native plantings that will absorb heat and control stormwater run-off.

Present-day Dodger Stadium

Ian Espinoza Associates

Dodger Stadium with Green Necklace development

Espinoza Associates

New outfield entrance

Green necklace

Top of the park

Appendix

Selected Works: Project Data

TALL BUILDINGS + URBAN HABITATS

MGM Tower
Century City, California
Completed 2003
704,000 gross sq. ft.
Client: JMB Realty
Contractor: Hathaway Dinwiddie
Structural engineer: WHL Consulting Engineers
MEP engineer: Levine Seegel Associates
Landscape architect: Mia Lehrer + Associates

Metropolitan Lofts
Los Angeles, California
Completed 2006
436,353 gross sq. ft.
Client: Forest City Residential West
Contractor: Keller Builders
Structural engineer: Nabih Youssef Associates
MP engineer: VLA Engineers, Inc.
Electrical engineer: Vorgias Consulting
Landscape architect: Mia Lehrer + Associates

Museum Tower
Dallas, Texas
In progress 2011
370,000 gross sq. ft.
Client: Brook Partners Inc. and Turtle Creek Holdings
Structural engineer: L.A. Fuess Partners
Landscape architect: Meléndrez

LeoPalace 21
Osaka, Japan
Design 2007–2009
360,000 sq. ft.
Client: LeoPalace 21
Engineers: Sumitomo Mitsui Construction Co., Ltd.

426 South Spring
Los Angeles, California
Design 2007–2008
200,000 gross sq. ft.
Client: Tom Gilmore and Goodwin Gaw
Structural engineer: Englekirk & Sabol Consulting Structural Engineers, Inc.
Landscape architect: Mia Lehrer + Associates

The Offices of Johnson Fain
Los Angeles, California
Completed 2004
26,919 gross sq. ft.
Client: Johnson Fain
Contractor: Minardos Builders
Structural engineers: Nabih Youssef Associates
MEP engineer: Levine Seegel Associates
Garden designer: Judy M. Horton Garden Design

PASTORAL LANDSCAPES

Opus One Winery
Oakville, California
Completed 1990
70,000 gross sq. ft.
Client: Opus One Winery
Construction management: L.E. Wentz Company
Engineers: The Bentley Company
Landscape architect: Royston Hanamoto Alley & Abbey

Byron Winery
Santa Maria Valley, California
Completed 1996
32,000 gross sq. ft.
Client: Robert Mondavi Winery
Contractor: BDM Construction Company, Inc.
Associate architect: Martinez & Associates
Structural engineer: Advanced Design Group, Inc.,
Refrigeration engineer: G.J. Fehlhaber, P. E.,
Electrical engineer: Gotham Light & Power
Landscape architect: Campbell & Campbell

The Clubhouse at Sandy Lane Resort
Saint James, Barbados
Completed 2001
55,000 gross sq. ft.
Client: International Investment & Underwriting, Ltd.
Structural engineer: Nabih Youssef Associates
MP Engineer: Leverage, Inc.
Electrical engineer: Kenderhall Enterprises Ltd.
Landscape architect: Tabora Tabora Blanco

Aetna Springs Clubhouse and Resort
Pope Valley, California
Completed 2008
8,800 gross sq. ft.
Client: Criswell Radovan Mondavi Getty
Contractor: Turner Construction
Structural engineer: Parker Resnik
Interior design: BraytonHughes Design Studios
Landscape architect: Smith+Smith

American Indian Cultural Center and Museum
Oklahoma City, Oklahoma
In progress 2010
125,000 gross sq. ft.
Client: Native American Cultural and Educational Authority
Contractor: Centennial Builders
Associate architect: Hornbeek Blatt Architects
Structural engineer: Nabih Youssef Associates
Civil engineer: Cardinal Engineering, Inc.
MEP engineer: IBE Consulting Engineers, Inc.
Landscape architect: Hargreaves Associates
Institutional planning: Lord Cultural Resources
Exhibit design: Ralph Appelbaum Associates

TECHNOLOGY, EDUCATION + RESEARCH

Amgen Building 27
Thousand Oaks, California
Completed 1997
230,000 gross sq. ft.
Client: Amgen
Contractor: Hathaway Dinwiddie
Structural engineer: Nabih Youssef Associates
MEP engineer: Levine Seegel Associates
Landscape architect: Meléndrez

Amgen Building 30
Thousand Oaks, California
Completed 2000
360,000 gross sq. ft.
Client: Amgen
Contractor: Hathaway Dinwiddie
Structural engineer: KPFF Consulting Engineers
MEP engineer: Bechtel Industrial and Affiliated
Engineers, Inc.
Landscape architect: Meléndrez
Lab planner: FLAD

Amgen Building 38
Thousand Oaks, California
Completed 2000
265,000 gross sq. ft.
Client: Amgen
Contractor: Hathaway Dinwiddie
Structural engineer: Nabih Youssef Associates
MEP engineer: Levine Seegel Associates
Landscape architect: Meléndrez

Genentech-32
South San Francisco, California
Completed 2004
125,387 gross sq. ft.
Client: Genentech
Contractor: Hathaway Dinwiddie
Structural engineer: Nabih Youssef Associates
Electrical engineer: KCA Engineers
Landscape architect: MPA Design

Genentech-33
South San Francisco, California
Completed 2005
130,115 gross sq. ft.
Client: Genentech
Contractor: Hathaway Dinwiddie
Structural engineer: Nabih Youssef Associates
Landscape architect: MPA Design

The Horizon
Playa Vista, Los Angeles, California
Completed 2009
950,000 gross sq. ft.
Client: Lincoln Property Company
Contractor: Morley Builders
Associate architect: HKS Architects, Inc.
Structural engineer: Saiful/Bouquet, Inc.
MEP engineer: ME Engineers, Inc.
Landscape architect: Rios Clementi Hale Studios

Cal(IT)²
Irvine, California
Completed 2004
120,000 gross sq. ft.
Client: University of California, Irvine
Contractor: PCL Construction Services
Associate architect: Leo A. Daly
Structural engineer: Nabih Youssef Associates
MP engineer: Capital Engineering
Electrical engineer: Levine Seegel Associates
Landscape architect: Meléndrez

Sutardja Dai Hall
Berkeley, California
Completed 2009
141,000 gross sq. ft.
Client: University of California, Berkeley
Contractor: Hathaway Dinwiddie
Associate architect: SmithGroup
Structural engineer: Forell/Elsesser Engineers, Inc.
MEP engineer: Bard, Rao + Athanas Consulting
Engineers, LLC
Landscape architect: KenKay Associates

Miguel Contreras Learning Complex
Los Angeles, California
Completed 2008
221,000 gross sq. ft.
Client: Los Angeles Unified School District
Contractor: Clark Construction Group, LLC
Structural engineer: Nabih Youssef Associates
MP engineer: William J. Yang & Associates
Electrical engineer: Silver, Roth & Associate, Inc.
Landscape architect: Mia Lehrer + Associates

Roy Romer Middle School
North Hollywood, California
Completed 2008
160,000 gross sq. ft.
Client: Los Angeles Unified School District
Contractor: Bernards
Structural engineer: Nabih Youssef Associates
MP engineer: William J. Yang & Associates
Electrical engineer: Silver, Roth & Associate, Inc.
Landscape architect: Mia Lehrer + Associates

HOUSES

Rutherford House
Rutherford, California
Completed 1999
4,200 sq. ft.
Contractor: Bachor Construction
Structural engineer: Parker Resnick
MEP engineer: M B & A
Landscape architect: Jack Chandler & Associates

St. Helena House
St. Helena, California
Completed 1994
3,600 sq. ft.
Contractor: Bachor Construction
Structural engineer: Nabih Youssef Associates
MEP engineer: Myron Kim
Landscape architect: Jack Chandler & Associates

Malibu House
Malibu, California
Completed 2003
8,000 gross sq. ft.
Contractor: Peregrine Inc.
Structural engineer: Parker Resnick
MEP engineer: M B & A
Landscape architect: Campbell & Campbell

Los Altos Hills House
Los Altos Hills, California
Completed 2001
6,800 gross sq. ft.
Contractor: Red Horse Constructors
Structural engineer: Lea & Sung Engineering
MEP engineer: Innovative Engineering Group , Inc.
Landscape designer: Nancy Goslee Power & Associates

Larchmont Village Townhouse
Los Angeles, California
Completed 2001
5,000 gross sq. ft.
Contractor: Minardos Builders
Structural engineer: Nabih Youssef Associates
MEP engineer: Innovative Engineering Group
Landscape designer: Judy M. Horton Garden Design

CIVIC SPACE

Capitol Area East End Complex
Sacramento, California
Completed 2003
1,500,000 gross sq. ft.
Client: State of California, Department of General
Services
Contractor: Clark Construction Group, LLC and Hensel
Phelps Construction Company
Associate architects: Gruen Architects, Fentress
Bradburn Architects, Dreyfuss & Blackford Architects,
SMWM Architects, and Forrar Williams Architects
Structural engineer: Middlebrook + Louie
MP engineer: Capital Engineering
Electrical engineer: Levine Seegel Associates
Landscape Architects: Meléndrez

Solano County Government Center
Fairfield, California
Completed 2005
300,000 gross sq. ft.
Client: County of Solano
Contractor: Clark Construction Group, LLC
Structural engineer, Nabih Youssef Associates
MP engineer: Capital Engineering Consultants
Electrical engineer: Levine Seegel Associates
Landscape architect: Meléndrez

Junipero Serra State Office Building
Los Angeles, California
Completed 1999
533,000 gross sq. ft.
Client: State of Califiornia, Department of General
Services
Contractor: Swinerton Builders
Structural engineer: John A. Martin & Associates
MEP engineer: Syska Hennessy Group, Inc.

Newport Beach City Hall
Newport Beach, California
Competition proposal 2008
79,000 sq. ft.
Client: City of Newport Beach
Landscape architect: Olin Partnership

Queensway Bay Parking Structure
Long Beach, California
Completed 1997
468,000 gross sq. ft.
1,500 spaces
Client: City of Long Beach
Contractor: Bomel Construction Company, Inc.
Parking design: International Parking Design

Dodger Stadium
Los Angeles, California
In progress 2012
350,000 sq. ft.
Client: The McCourt Group, Inc.
Associate architect: HKS Architects, Inc.
Structural engineer: Nabih Youssef Associates
MEP engineer: Syska Hennessy Group
Landscape architect: Rios Clementi Hale Studios, HRP
Studio, and Comstock Studio

Project Sponsors

ABC
Allied Communications
American Airlines
Amgen
Apollo Real Estate Advisors
Barker Pacific
Beacon Capital Management
Bear Stearns
Beijing Central Business District Planning Committee
Beijing LangFang Jing Yu Real Estate Co., Ltd.
Best Land Property
Boeing Realty
Broadway Partners
Brook Partners, Inc.
Byron Winery
California Institute of Technology
James Campbell Company
Catellus Development
CBS Television City
Century Plaza Hotel
Chadwick School
Chengdu BRC Group
Chengdu LongQuan Yi District Government
Chengdu ShuangLiu Urban Planning Administration Bureau
Chengdu WideHorizon Investment Co., Ltd.
Chengdu Wide Horizon Real Estate Development Co., Ltd.
Chinese Embassy
City National Bank
City of Beverly Hills
City of Culver City
City of Fullerton
City of Indian Wells
City of Irvine
City of Long Beach
City of Los Angeles
Commonwealth Partners
Conexant
Country of Saudia Arabia
County of Los Angeles
County of Solano
Criswell Radovan
Development Management Associates

DreamWorks SKG
E. & J. Gallo Winery
East Los Angeles College
Experian
Fairplex
Fairs Lee Investments
Fangshan University
Fashion Institute of Design and Merchandising
Folio Wines
Foothill Transit
Forest City Development
Forest City Residential West
Four Media
Genentech
Gerding Edlen
Gilead
Giorgio
Gooden Estate
Guangzhou Development Area Planning and Construction Bureau
Hillcrest Country Club
Hilton Hotels
Hines
InfoMart
International Investment & Underwriting, Ltd.
JARCO LLC
Jet Propulsion Laboratory
JLM Realty
JMB Realty
JMI
Jones Lang LaSalle
JSB Development
Kamehameha Schools
KB Home
KNBC / Telemundo
Legacy Partners
Lennar
Lieff Estate
LNR
Lincoln Properties Group
Lockheed Corporation
Los Altos Hills Estate
Los Angeles Area Chamber of Commerce

Los Angeles Center Studios
Los Angeles Community College District
Los Angeles Country Club
Los Angeles County Museum of Art
Los Angeles County Natural History Museum
Los Angeles Dodgers
Los Angeles Times
Los Angeles Unified School District
Los Angeles World Airports
LuoJiang City Government
Mapleton Securities
Marlborough School
Marriott
MCA / Universal
McCarthy • Cook
Mission College
Mitchell Energy Corp.
Molasky Pacific
Native American Cultural and Educational Authority
NBC / Universal
Nestle USA
Newhall Land & Farming
New Urban West
Norton Air Force Base
Opus One Winery
Otis Art Institute
Pacific Properties
Paradise Restaurant
Paramount Studios
Pepperdine University
Pierce College
Platt College
Playa Capital
Racke USA
Robert Mondavi Winery
San Jose Redevelopment Agency
Shanghai Chia Chun Real Estate Corporation
Shanghai SongJiang District Government
Shanghai Urban Construction Investment and
    Development General Corporation
Sheraton Hotels
Sichuan LangJiu Group
St. Andrews Abbey

St. Paul's Cathedral
Stadco
State of California, Department of General Services
SunAmerica
SunCal Companies
Sunkist
The Clarett Group
The McCourt Group, Inc.
The Mills Corporation
The Ratkovich Company
The Staubach Company
Thomas Safran & Associates
Ticketmaster
Tishman International
Toyota Motor Sales USA
Trump Organization
Turtle Creek Holdings
Twentieth Century Fox
Twenty-First Century Insurance
Union Bank
United States General Services Administration
Universal Studios
University of California Berkeley
University of California Irvine
University of California Los Angeles
University of California Riverside
University of California San Diego
University of California Santa Barbara
University of Southern California
University of Southern California Keck School of Medicine
Unocal
Urban Partners
Urban Retail Properties
V2 Ventures
Warner Bros.
Whittier College
William Morris Rodeo
Williams & Dame
Wilshire Country Club
YCS Investments
YMCA
Young Nak Church of Los Angeles

Design Team

John Adams
Barron E Allen
David J Alpaugh – *Associate Principal*
S Morteza Alvani – *Senior Associate*
Karla L Amber
Mili Amin
Kristen M Anderson
Paul H Anvar – *Associate*
Corina Apodaca
Larry R Ball – *Principal*
Julie W Bandini
Juan C Begazo – *Principal*
Maria O Bento
Venke Blyberg
Mark J Borkowski
Grace Bou
Tom Brakefield – *Associate*
Sean Briski
Sangeeta Bulani – *Associate*
Sandra Burga
Benjamin T Campana
Jessica S Campion
Gokhan Caydamli
Joy T Chan
Michael Chan
Bruce Chan
Eddie Char
Shih-Pu Nora Chen
Pakling Chiu
Hyeyoon Chung
Linda T Chung
Steve Chung
Matthew A Conway
Agnes Corrales
Michelle B Costa Baron
Joanne Costello
Kershasp E Dalal – *Senior Associate*
Philip M De Cancio – *Associate*
Carlos G Delgado
Margie A Dianco
Pearl M Diggs
James E Donaldson – *Associate*
Daniel Elkins
William H. Fain, Jr. – *Partner*

Mary Faria
Jack Fong
Tina Forrestel
Edith Fortea
Jeffrey Fox
Melissa Francis
Syou-Ling Fu
Christina M Fujii
Garine Gabrielian
Amalia Gal
Andrew Galambos
Lawrence E Garcia
Douglas J Gardner
Soheir Georges
Mark R Gershen – *Principal*
Todd D Gish
Manuel Gonzales
Pierpaolo Granata
Trina M Gunther
Joel Hernandez
Megumi Hironaka
Adela Ho
Erik O Hovlin
India Howlett
Jeanette Hsu
Po Yuan H Huang
Cameron Izuno
Adriana Mora-Jackson
James Jackson
John G M Jackson
Daniel J Janotta – *Principal*
Cynthia A Johnson
Maxwell Johnson
Scott Johnson – *Partner*
Mohan P Joshi
Neil M Kaplanis
Mieun Kim
Steven H Klausner
Anne E Koshalek
Jacques Kravtchenko
Carter G Larson
Karen Lee
Kenny Lee
Edward Lee

Jaewon Lee
Sahng O Lee
Anson Lesmana
Jeffrey A Levy
Benjamin Liao
Chien-Hui Lin
Marci L Loftin
Dawna Lough
Jenny Mach
Kavita R Mahabaleshwark
Hung Mak
Edwin Q Maldonado
Victor Malerba, Jr.
Abhijeet D Mankar – *Principal*
William Martin, Jr.
Michael E McCarthy
Shannon A McShea
Cherie D Miller
Akira Nakano
Cynthia L O'Bleness
Grace C. Oh
Rigoberto Ortega
Carlo Paganuzzi
Guy Painchaud
Jennifer Pascoe
Andrea Pavia
Alejandro Pijuan
Neda Pourshakouri
Gig Pukprayura
Lorenz Quinley
Raymond Rangel
Victor Raskovsky
Ian Y Remulla – *Senior Associate*
Irlanda E Rendon
Arnold A Rivera
Chea Seon Roh – *Associate*
Daniel Romo
Joel M Rosenberg
Liza B Rossi
Francois Ruel
Peter Ruppel
Kelly Ryan
Sepideh Salehirad
Steven Sato

In Young Seo
Robert P Shaffer – *Associate Principal*
Samir Shaikh
Patricia Shigetomi – *Principal*
Cynthia Simonian
Mark A Skiles
Stephen Slaughter
Dana Smith – *Senior Associate*
Kyle Smith
John Son
Jennifer A Spangler
Suma Spina
James Stafford
Arnold Swanborn
Kenji Tanaka
Scott Taylor
Wichai Thanavatik
Priyanka D Thatte
Sandra Torres
Erik Valderrama
Elena Valderrama – *Associate Principal*
Cecilia Valino
Gregory Verabian – *Principal*
Anna T Villanueva
Loann H Vu
Li-Hsin Wang
Eric S Weeks
Yu-Ming Wei
Aran T Weng
Patrick J Wildnauer
Serena Y Winner
Janice Wong
Allen D Wong
Li Wu
Donald Yamami
Jui-Ni Yang
Jenny P Yee
Vivian Yeung
Hai-yan Yu
Nanita Yung
Holly M Zeiler
Hraztan Zeitlian
Chunyan Zhang – *Senior Associate*

Photo Credits

Miguel Contreras Learning Complex (132–139)
Benny Chan/Fotoworks, pages 132–133, 135–138
Lawrence Anderson, page 134

Roy Romer Middle School (140–145)
All photos by Benny Chan/Fotoworks

HOUSES
Rutherford House (148–153)
Tom Bonner, page 150 left, 153 top
Tim Griffith, pages 148–149, 150–151, 152
Erhard Pfeiffer, page 153 bottom

St. Helena House (154–159)
Erhard Pfeiffer, pages 156 right, 157, 159
Tim Street Porter, pages 154, 156 left, 158

Malibu House (160–169)
All photos by Tom Bonner

Los Altos Hills House (170–177)
Erhard Pfeiffer, pages 170, 173, 174–177

Larchmont Village Townhouse (178–185)
Russell Abraham, pages 178–179
Erhard Pfeiffer, page 184
Tim Street-Porter, pages 181, 182, 183, 185

CIVIC SPACE
Capitol Area East End Complex (188–197)
Digital sky, page 192 top
Erhard Pfeiffer, pages 188, 190, 191, 192 bottom, 194–197
Richard Ross, page 193

Solano County Government Center (198–203)
Tim Griffith, page 200
Michael O'Callahan, pages 198, 201, 202, 203

Junipero Serra State Office Building (204–207)
All photos by Mark Lohman

Newport Beach City Hall + Park (208–215)
Ian Espinoza, pages 210, 211
Mark Lohman, pages 208, 214, 215

Queensway Bay Parking Structure (216–221)
Erhard Pfeiffer, pages 216, 218, 220, 221

Dodger Stadium (222–227)
Tom Bonner, pages 222, 227 right
Ian Espinoza, pages 225, 226, 227 left

Acknowledgements

While the creation of a book like this tends to be driven by a simple long-term vision, it is necessarily a complex, somewhat amorphous production effort. I thank everyone for their forbearance. I wish to thank, in particular, my partner and colleague, Bill Fain, for his enlightened contributions in the office and his enthusiastic support for projects that extend our borders. Together with Bill, I must thank our experienced and energetic staff, chief among them, the principals, Larry Ball, Juan Begazo, Mark Gershen, Dan Janotta, Abhijeet Mankar, Patsy Shigetomi, and Greg Verabian. Working closely with all of us at Johnson Fain are the many consultants and creative collaborators who participate at the center of the design process.

For making specific contributions to the production of this book, my thanks go to Greg Verabian for organizing much of the materials, to Bruce Chan for assembly of same, to Mark Gershen and Dana Smith for support and, in particular, their intelligent review of texts, to India Howlett for making available to this venture her graphic design talents, and to Cherie Miller, my assistant, for putting up with and supporting the creation of yet another book. This project would not exist without the support and fine contributions of Paul Latham, Alessina Brooks, and the knowledgeable team at The Images Publishing Group, our publishers in Melbourne, Australia.

Finally, I wish to thank Joseph Giovannini for his thoughtful and expansive foreword to the book.

—*Scott Johnson*